INVESTIGATING THE INFORMATION SOCIETY

The Open University course team

Tracey Allen, *Project Officer*

Geoff Andrews, *Lecturer and Staff Tutor in Politics*

Sally Baker, *Subject Information Specialist
(Education and Social Sciences)*

John Bennett, *Course Manager*

Pam Berry, *Compositor*

Tom Burden, *Consultant*

Stephen Clift, *Editor*

Rob Clifton, *Lecturer and Staff Tutor in Politics*

Lene Connolly, *Print Buying Controller*

Jonathan Davies, *Graphic Designer*

Lesley Duguid, *Senior Course Co-ordination Secretary*

Janet Fink, *Lecturer in Social Policy*

John Hunt, *Project Officer, Social Sciences*

Margaret Kiloh, *Course Team Chair, Senior Lecturer and
Staff Tutor in Social Policy*

Hugh Mackay, *Senior Lecturer and Staff Tutor in Sociology*

Wendy Maples, *Lecturer and Staff Tutor in Geography*

Michelle Perrott, *Assistant Librarian, Learner Support
(Education and Social Sciences)*

Paul Reynolds, *Consultant*

Diana Shore, *Learning Technologist*

Colin Thomas, *Software Designer*

Emma Wheeler, *Production and Presentation Administrator*

External Assessor

Frank Webster, *Professor of Sociology, University of Birmingham*

INVESTIGATING THE INFORMATION SOCIETY

Hugh Mackay

with
Wendy Maples

and
Paul Reynolds

Routledge
Taylor & Francis Group
New York   London

This book forms part of the Open University course DXR220 *Social Science in Action: Investigating the Information Society*. Details of this and other Open University courses can be obtained from the Call Centre, PO Box 724, The Open University, Milton Keynes MK7 6ZS, United Kingdom: tel. +44 (0)1908 653231, e-mail cesgen@open.ac.uk

Alternatively, you may visit the Open University website at http://www.open.ac.uk where you can learn more about the wide range of courses and packs offered at all levels by The Open University.

For availability of other course components, contact Open University Worldwide Ltd, The Berrill Building, Walton Hall, Milton Keynes MK7 6AA, United Kingdom: tel. +44 (0)1908 858785; fax +44 (0)1908 858787; e-mail ouwenq@open.ac.uk; website http://www.ouw.co.uk

First published 2001 by Routledge; written and produced by The Open University
2 Park Square, Milton Park, Abingdon, Oxon OX14 4RN

Simultaneously published in the USA and Canada by Routledge
711 Third Avenue, New York, NY 10017

Routledge is an imprint of the Taylor & Francis Group

© 2001 The Open University

Edited, designed and typeset by The Open University.

British Library Cataloguing in Publication Data
A catalogue record for this book is available from The British Library

Library of Congress Cataloging in Publication Data
A catalogue record for this book has been requested

ISBN 0-415-26831-1 (hbk)

ISBN 0-415-26832-X (pbk)

1.2

CONTENTS

PREFACE

Investigating the Information Society has been written as an introduction to debates about the information society and, at the same time, to introduce a breadth of social science research methods. It has been written as the core text for the 15 point Open University level 2 course DXR220, which has the same title as this book. The course is something of a bold and innovative response to some of the requirements of subject benchmarking in UK higher education, addressing some of the most pressing intellectual debates of our time and outlining the practices of social scientists in exploring these.

We use 'the information society' as an umbrella term for some important contemporary social transformations that are underway. So the book and the course will appeal to anyone trying to make sense of the emerging social order and, especially, the three core themes of information society debates that are identified and explored in some depth: culture, representations and identities; changing work and inequalities; and time–space reconfiguration. Thus, the empirical focus of the book is designed to have a broad appeal across many of the social science subjects. It introduces and evaluates critically some core claims about the contemporary social order.

At the same time, the book outlines some core methods and methodologies of social science research. As well as providing an account of the development of social science research methods, it explores ways in which the research process is itself profoundly social by addressing questions of objectivity and reflexivity. In introducing both issues and techniques for deploying a breadth of core research methods, it will equip you to gather and process your own data, to become, in a preliminary way, a social researcher. Many research studies are introduced for their substantive contribution to debates about the information society, but these are also evaluated in terms of the criteria by which social scientists assess research.

Open University courses are produced by course teams that include academic authors, from within and beyond The Open University, tutors, an External Assessor, editors, designers, BBC producers, academic computing specialists, administrators and secretaries. Many members of the DXR220 course team have contributed to this volume, and other colleagues in the Faculty of Social Sciences have supported our development of the course and this book, so it is awkward to single out a few for special mention. Nonetheless, I should like to acknowledge Margaret Kiloh, Course Chair, who has steered the project through the OU machine, provided incisive comments, and kept everyone calm. Frank Webster, our External Assessor, has provided critical but supportive comments on the breadth of course materials. Lesley Duguid, secretary, has been assiduous and speedy at processing numerous drafts, even when we got them mixed up. Stephen Clift, editor, has been invaluably ruthless about deadlines and wordcounts, as well as a judicious editor. Finally, eleven students from the OU's social sciences level 1 course spent a week working through a draft of this book and the associated residential course, and the course team is grateful for their dedication to this task and the inspiration they provided.

We hope that you will find the book engaging, and that it will stimulate and inform your interest in the information society. We hope it will equip you to evaluate the claims that are made by researchers and others about the transformations that are underway, and enable you to begin to conduct your own social research.

Hugh Mackay
The Open University

Introduction

Hugh Mackay

The information society is how contemporary social transformation is commonly conceived. It is a loose umbrella term, used by various authors and commentators to refer to far-reaching social change that is underway. It encompasses a diversity of arguments, which all see information, and information technology, as somehow lying at the heart of the emerging social order. Greater volumes of information are being communicated by a fast-growing range of technologies with profound social consequences. These consequences can be identified in nearly every aspect of social life.

Three themes can be identified in information society debates. First is the rise to the fore of culture, reflected in the growth in the ownership and use of a range of cultural technologies. From the dawn of television broadcasting around the time of the Second World War, to the multi-channel world of cable and satellite, digital, wide-screen, high-definition and interactive television about half a century later, is a dramatic transformation. And as well as television there is video, the cinema, music, periodicals and books. Nor is this confined to the media: through advertising, the telephone, the Internet, photography, clothing and the artefacts in our homes, we are dealing with an ever-increasing array of information and images. This is not simply a question of volume. The interaction surrounding these media, technologies and activities occupy a major part of our daily lives, and our identities increasingly come to be constructed by, and expressed through, what we consume. As the world becomes increasingly saturated with signs, they become (as Baudrillard and other postmodernists argue) increasingly self-referential: it is increasingly difficult to identify *simulations* as something separate from reality in a world described by Baudrillard as hyper-reality. Image, 'spin' and scepticism become prevalent and taken-for-granted.

Second is the changing economy, the changing nature of work, and changing patterns of inequality. It's not difficult to understand that work is changing – with the decline of employment in not just coal and steel, but manufacturing generally, and of service employment, and the rise of information work. Economists and sociologists have examined industrial and occupational classifications, and have identified and enumerated these trends. The argument is that there has been a huge growth in industrialized countries of information work. More than this, the strategic *significance* of information industries and occupations has been recognized. In other words, they are not just growing, but they are the cornerstones of the economy – in a symbolic as well as strategic sense. In the process, it is argued, we are witnessing the re-ordering of the social structure: power and status is being distributed in new ways, with new winners and losers. Access to information and

ICTs

ICTs are information technologies (ITs), but as a term is often used to give more emphasis to social, rather than technical, aspects of communication.

communication technologies (**ICTs**), and to information, both reflects and reinforces social divisions, with a growing polarization between those with access to information and the 'information have-nots'

Finally, there is the spatial and temporal dimension: with the spread and growing significance of ICTs we are experiencing the reconfiguration of time and space. Increasingly, information networks mean that time and space become less significant in shaping social organization and interaction. The electronic infrastructure allows real-time coordination across the globe in ways, and with consequences, that were unthinkable until recently. Financial systems and trading operate across national borders with increasing ease and speed. Production, marketing and coordination increasingly span the world as we become integrated in a global economy, polity and culture. Although not a monolithic, unilinear or homogenizing process, we are seeing the emergence of new networks and new links between organizations, nations and regions. In the process, and with the vast capacity of the communication networks, time in some senses becomes insignificant: real-time data, such as video pictures, can be transmitted instantly across the globe by satellite, while e-mail replaces airmail.

How are we to make sense of such transformations? There is no shortage of commentators – including politicians, journalists and futurists – who refer to the social upheaval that characterizes contemporary society. Some of their arguments are forceful and provocative, and they commonly invoke data to illustrate or sustain their conclusions.

Social scientists comment on similar issues, and often with similar arguments. Whilst we can identify a great diversity of approaches within the social sciences, from positivism to postmodernism, there are important ways in which social science differs from most other analyses of the information society.

This book provides an introduction to some key issues and practices of doing social research. It aims to introduce social science in action. Social scientists seek to understand the social through the use of research methods, or techniques, of gathering data. Social science data take many forms and are collected in many ways, including by questionnaire surveys, interviews and textual analysis. In this book we shall introduce each of these, and other research methods.

Research methods are not selected in a vacuum, or arbitrarily, from those available. Rather, particular methods are associated with particular theoretical approaches to making sense of society. Such perspectives deploy concepts and theories to make sense of data and to link data to argument or explanation. In the social sciences a number of such methodologies (as distinct from methods) can be identified. In this book we explore the central tenets of four of these: positivist, interpretivist, critical and cultural. Each is associated with a particular understanding of what we can know about the social world and the limits and possibilities of social science research and knowledge. They provide a framework for the deployment of methods, the collection of data and the development of arguments.

This book aims to add to the experience of reading social science by introducing research methods and methodologies which provide a framework for evaluating and undertaking research on the information society.

In relation to the three core themes of information society debates which we have identified – the growth of culture and rise to the fore of the symbolic, the restructuring of work and changing patterns of inequality, and the reconfiguration of time and space – we introduce some key ideas. We then evaluate specific research studies in each area, in terms of their validity, reliability, comprehensiveness and coherence. Of these criteria of evaluation, validity and reliability relate more to data, and comprehensiveness and coherence are more applicable to argument. Rather than universal criteria – which can be applied in a similar way to all research – each is more or less applicable to particular studies, depending on their methodology. By deploying these criteria we can evaluate the strengths and limits of a range of empirical studies of the information society.

Chapter 1 provides a broad introduction to the information society by introducing the discourse of the information society and considering what it means in the home, at work, for warfare and for surveillance. These are four somewhat arbitrary areas, selected to give a flavour of the transformations implicated in information society debates.

Chapter 2 is more detailed and specific. It explores the work of two social scientists who, probably more than any others, have defined the parameters of information society debates – the sociologist Daniel Bell and the urban theorist Manuel Castells. Bell wrote in the 1970s of the coming 'post-industrial society' (which in his later work he called the 'information society'). By this he meant that Western economies were experiencing a decline of employment in manufacturing and the growth of the service and information sectors, in a process commonly known as de-industrialization. Perhaps strangely for a sociologist, Bell saw technology as the driving force of history. This is the position known as technological determinism, which is a common way of conceiving of the relationship between technology and society, and one that we explore in some depth. We then move to the work of Castells, who provides an account of today's 'network society', in which space and time are virtually eliminated by the new electronic networks. New technologies, capitalist restructuring and a growing concern about identity have combined to give rise to a new form of society, and one which, for Castells, offers exciting possibilities for new politics.

Having outlined information society debates, in Chapter 3 we introduce some key aspects of social science research methods. We contrast social science with common-sense thinking, and explore the relationship between theory, data and values in the research process. We introduce various categories of data: primary and secondary, and qualitative and quantitative. We introduce and discuss the four criteria for evaluating social science research which we deploy later: validity, reliability, comprehensiveness and coherence.

We examine the philosophical underpinnings of social research methods in Chapter 4. The chapter addresses research methodologies – the approaches to social science understanding that lie behind any research project and research design. Methodologies are rooted in approaches to understanding what social science knowledge and understanding can be generated. We also discuss particular research tools, or methods of research, that are commonly deployed by proponents of each of the four methodologies – positivist, interpretivist, critical and cultural. In something of a historical account, we explain that there has been a shift from approaches which see social science as capable of generating social facts, or laws (rather akin to common understandings of natural science), to approaches which foreground the contingent, contested, subjective and cultural nature of social understanding. Notions of objective truths are a far cry from the deconstruction associated with discourse analysis.

Having outlined some key issues about methods and methodologies, in Chapters 5, 6 and 7 we apply these ideas to particular empirical studies of aspects of the information society. Each of these chapters deals with one of the three core themes of information society debates that we have identified – the growth of culture and rise to the fore of the symbolic, the restructuring of work and changing patterns of inequality, and the reconfiguration of time and space. Each provides an account of the scope of research and arguments in relation to the theme. Each then introduces and evaluates a small number of relevant research projects in the area, drawing on the four criteria of evaluation – validity, reliability, comprehensiveness and coherence.

Chapter 5 introduces and explores debates about culture, representation and identity. It considers the growth of the media and of the significance of culture, the increasing saturation of society with images and symbols, and the significance for the information society of new possibilities and senses of identity. The methods of textual and discourse analysis, semiotics and deconstruction are introduced in evaluating research studies of World Wide Web homepages and other forms of computer-mediated communication.

Chapter 6 is concerned with the restructuring of work (building on the work of Daniel Bell, explored in Chapter 2) and changing patterns of inequality. New technologies and other factors have led to the dramatic transformation of virtually every job, organization and sector, and the growth of the 'e-economy'. Various aspects of these changes are introduced to provide a picture of the changing nature of work. In these processes there have been winners and losers, and debates about 'information-haves' and 'have-nots' are introduced.

Chapter 7 addresses the third and final of the three core themes of information society debates, the reconfiguration of time and space. Building on the work of Manuel Castells (introduced in Chapter 2) it explores aspects of new connections and networks that are facilitated by new ICTs. With time and space virtually annihilated, boundaries are breached and new patterns of association emerge, with profound consequences for communities, nations and identities.

A short conclusion links the various issues explored, and considers the relevance of social science for understanding the information society.

Investigating the Information Society introduces both debates about the information society and the practices of social research. It will equip you with an understanding of some issues that are involved in collecting and analysing data and constructing arguments in the social sciences. It is an introduction to research methods and methodologies, and it provides an explanation of the contribution of social science to our understanding of the information society.

The information society: continuity or change?

chapter 1

Hugh Mackay

● ●

1 THE INFORMATION SOCIETY DISCOURSE

Social scientists have commonly sought to understand the major social transformations underway at their time of writing – notably the work of Karl Marx on industrialization, Emile Durkheim's concern with social stability, and Max Weber's analysis of bureaucracy. Contemporary social transformation in the developed world has led social scientists to seek to understand what many have called the information society. It's likely that you have heard of this notion because in the press, on radio and television, in popular culture, literature, industry, education, official reports and social research we find claims of far-reaching social transformations referred to in terms of an emerging information society. Other terms in circulation – post-industrial society, network society and knowledge society, for example – carry similar or overlapping meanings. The term 'information society' spans the social and the technical: the global information infrastructure, the Internet, the World Wide Web, the e-economy, information technology (IT), telecommunications, digitization, **convergence**, and many more. Although there is considerable variation in analysis of the social, economic and political significance of the information society, together these debates form a **discourse**, a set of ideas, concepts and understandings that are invoked in a diversity of contexts. Crucial, as we shall see, is the growth of information and IT.

Nicholas Negroponte, Director of the Media Laboratory at Massachusetts Institute of Technology, is a leading commentator on the digital future. His book, *Being Digital*, draws on his columns in the monthly magazine *Wired*, and constitutes a typical perspective within the broad information society discourse:

> Early in the next millennium your right or left cufflinks or earrings may communicate with each other by low-orbiting satellites and have more computer power than your present PC. Your telephone won't ring

Convergence
This term relates to the technical (telecommunicating and computing), the content (graphics, sound and text on the Internet), and the medium (e.g. radio on the Internet).

Discourse
A narrative in which a set of concepts, unified by common assumptions, is brought together.

indiscriminately; it will receive, sort and perhaps respond to your incoming calls like a well-trained English butler. Mass media will be redefined by systems for transmitting and receiving personalized information and entertainment. Schools will change to become more like museums and playgrounds for children to assemble ideas and socialize with other children all over the world. The digital planet will look and feel like the head of a pin.

(Negroponte, 1995, p.6)

In a similar vein, the futurist Tom Stonier argues that 'modern productive systems no longer depend on land, labour and capital as their primary input; rather, they require information' (Stonier, 1983, p.306). Such analysis is not, however, confined to futurists. Mark Poster, a communications theorist, argues that 'new forms of social interaction based on electronic communications devices are replacing older types of social relations' (Poster, 1984, p.168). As an oral culture was replaced by print, so this is being replaced by electronic communication (Poster, 1990). David Bolter, a classicist with an interest in computing, argues that, in the same way as the clock is the symbol of the industrial era, the computer occupies 'a special place in our cultural landscape. It is the technology that more than any other defines our age ... giving us a new definition of man, as an "information processor", and of nature, as "information to be processed"' (Bolter, 1986, pp.8–9, 13).

The 'information society' is prominent too in a breadth of government and European Union (EU) policies. Martin Bangemann, European Commissioner and Head of the European Council Directorate General XIII, led a 'high-level group' of 'prominent persons' that reported to the European Council in 1994 on the measures the EC and its member states should consider regarding information infrastructure. His report was unambiguous in its analysis of the present as the time of an information revolution:

> Throughout the world, information and communications technologies are generating a new industrial revolution already as significant and far-reaching as those of the past.
>
> It is a revolution based on information ...
>
> This revolution adds huge new capacities to human intelligence and constitutes a resource which changes the way we work together and live together. ...
>
> All revolutions generate uncertainty, discontinuity – and opportunity. Today's is no exception. How we respond, how we turn current opportunities into real benefits, will depend on how quickly we can enter the European information society.
>
> (Bangemann, 1994, ch.1)

This analysis has been used to inform a raft of EU policies, including the development of a regulatory framework for infrastructure and services, the stimulation of technology research and applications, increasing public awareness of the information society and monitoring its social and cultural impacts. These policies seek to stimulate both production and consumption, within the context of the free market and private sector investment. Many areas of EU intervention, including its funding of regional economic development, lie under its 'information society' umbrella.

In the USA you can find a similar concern, though commonly couched in terms of the 'information superhighway', a notion associated closely with Al Gore. For him, the global information infrastructure (GII) is:

> a planetary information network that transmits messages and images with the speed of light from the largest city to the smallest village on every continent ... The GII will circle the globe with information superhighways on which all people can travel ... These highways – or, more accurately, networks of distributed intelligence – will allow us to share information, to connect, and to communicate as a global community. From these connections we will derive robust and sustainable economic progress, strong democracies, better solutions to global and local environmental challenges, improved health care and – ultimately – a greater sense of stewardship of our small planet ... Hundreds of billions of dollars can be added to world growth if we commit to the GII.
>
> (speech to the International Telecommunication Union World Telecommunication Development Conference, Buenos Aires, 21 March 1994)

Nearer home we can find similar sentiments and policies, with both Conservative and Labour governments committed to using IT to improve communication between citizens and the government. At the time of writing the Cabinet Office has a Central IT Unit, the PM has an MP as his e-Envoy and there is an e-Minister. The 10 Downing Street website (http://www.number-10.gov.uk) provides information about the Prime Minister and the government. A related e-mail service allows citizens to be updated regarding government activities in which they have expressed an interest. This is not simply a one-way channel for funnelling official information. Rather, the idea is a two-way process, in which dialogue, sharing knowledge, and involvement and participation are facilitated. The 10 Downing Street website allows feedback, as the PM's welcome statement outlines: 'this site lets you have your say. Take part in a discussion forum, or pose a question to be asked in one of our live broadcasts'. Visitors to the site can observe discussions which are underway, make their own contributions to these, or even open up new topics for discussion.

ACTIVITY 1.1

Log on to 10 Downing Street. If you do not have easy Internet access, try to get a friend to help, or get to an Internet café. Log on to 10 Downing Street (http://www.number-10.gov.uk) and view a discussion. What do you see as the strengths and limits of such government sites, as regards extending democracy and participation?

COMMENT _____

This Internet site appears to represent a new and significant channel for enabling expression of opinion by citizens to government, with some indication of discussion being taken seriously (at the time when we looked, there was a summary by the PM of a discussion which had taken place). But how many can contribute to such discussion? Who are they? Who is *not* contributing, and why do you think they are not? What is the significance for those who are excluded of others taking advantage of the access allowed and possibly influencing policies? Who is organizing, ordering and managing the discussion? What do you think is happening when a discussion is summarized? More broadly, in what ways does such electronic access transform democracy?

_____

However trivial or transformatory you feel it is for the government to offer such access, the rhetoric that surrounds the development of such services is very much in the 'information society' mould, and part of a long-established tradition. It is about two decades since John Naisbett argued that the USA shifted from an industrial to an information society in the 1960s or 1970s (Naisbett, 1982); since Alvin Toffler referred to an 'information bomb' exploding in our midst and of a power shift in society as a consequence of its increased dependence on knowledge (Toffler, 1980); or since Tom Stonier saw the dawning of a new age which was as different from the industrial period as that was from the Middle Ages (Stonier, 1983). Indeed, one of the best known and most elaborate accounts of the information society remains the work of an American sociologist Daniel Bell, who wrote of the 'post-industrial society' in the 1960s. His post-industrial society has similar features to the 'information society' (Bell, 1974). We shall examine Bell's work in some detail in Chapter 2.

Data
Data are information, but without any claims for truth or validity.

All of these commentators outline significant and substantial changes to society. Each, in different ways and using different sources, provides a range of **data** to support their claims, including their own observations, published statistics and the evidence of experts. They see the emergence of an information society as something supported by data.

ACTIVITY 1.2

Find some data of your own on the growth of information. If you have access to the Internet, this will be a useful source – you could try the World Telecommunication Development Report at http://www.itu.ch/WTDR95/. If not, a quality newspaper will be a useful source.

COMMENT _____

The source cited tells us that:

- The global information sector is growing faster than overall economic growth.

- The information sector appears less susceptible to economic downswings, e.g. whilst the global economy contracted by 3.3% in 1991, the information industry grew by 6%.

- The contribution of the information sector to the global economy is expanding, and stood at 5.6% in 1993. This represents US$1,352 billion.

- In the USA, the share of household budget spent on information rose from 9.9% to 12.5%, while the proportion spent on food declined from 19.9% to 16.5% between 1980 and 1992.

- In 1994 the value of the European information sector was US$329 billion and growth was forecast at 6% per annum for 1995 and 1996.

- In Japan the info-communications sector's share of the national economy rose from 5.8% in 1980 to 9.5% in 1992, when it was valued at US$683 billion.

- In the USA, employment in the computer software industry has almost tripled since the advent of personal computing.

- From 1992 to 2005, demand for computer programmers/analysts is forecast to double. It will be the second fastest growing occupation after home care workers.

2   THE INFORMATION SOCIETY?

This is one example of the abundance of data that supports the notion that there has been a dramatic growth of information, the information industries and information technology. For many commentators, it is a small shift from reading these data to arguing that it represents substantial social, economic, cultural and political transformation – changing households, work, democracy and even how we see ourselves, our identities. Such accounts, however, raise several issues. First, explanations of the information society are not all the same, so which do we regard as the best? How do we interpret their claims and their significance? How do we evaluate the different views and explain our reasons for preferring one to another? How do we evaluate their different arguments and uses of data? Second, what does it mean to say that society is transforming, and information and information and communication technologies (ICTs) are at its heart? Is the change superficial or profound? How important is it compared with the continuities in society, culture, politics and the economy? In short, how do we make sense of the information society?

As we shall see, there are many different authors and theorists who use the term 'information society' and, commonly, they use it to refer to different phenomena. They are referring to a new kind of society, one which has to be understood in new terms, which begs some new social analysis or understanding. Beyond this, however, there is considerable variation – and, often, a lack of clarity – in what is being discussed.

ICTs are transforming virtually every area of social life. We can't explore all of these, but we start this chapter by exploring four areas in which major social changes relating to new technologies can be identified. The selection of these four areas is fairly arbitrary – the home, work, the military, and surveillance – and the idea is to outline the scope of some of the transformations which are underway to give a flavour of the information society.

3   THE INFORMATION SOCIETY IN FOUR ARENAS

As well as a discourse, the information society is something we all experience: it is not simply a set of debates. So what does the 'information society' mean to you? *In what ways* are we living in an information society?

We are all in different positions and have different experiences in our everyday lives. But no doubt you have been able to identify *some* aspects of the information society in your life. By way of starting to think about the scope of the information society, we shall explore briefly four areas in which new technologies seem to be linked to profound social change. You should take these case studies as indicative of the broader phenomenon of the information society.

3.1 The home

In the home, we have seen dramatic transformations in which IT has been central. From the end of the nineteenth century, but mostly in the early twentieth century, a series of infrastructural and service technologies was introduced: running water, electricity and gas, together with associated appliances, notably lights, cookers, boilers, refrigerators, washing machines and dishwashers, and a panoply of smaller devices – electric irons, toasters, coffee makers, etc. Those we have named can all be labelled 'work' technologies, known as 'white goods' in the retail trade. The other area of growth is in 'brown goods', or leisure technologies. Starting with the telephone (late nineteenth century), the gramophone (around the same time), the wireless (in the 1920s), and the television (briefly and on a small scale before the Second World War, and then again after the war), the home today is saturated with leisure ICTs.

ACTIVITY 1.3

Make a list of leisure technologies in *your* home. Who is the main user and when?

C O M M E N T

I came up with the following in my house:

- a computer used for work, the Internet, and for playing CDs (also used by the children for e-mail games and homework)
- a cable service which supplies telephony (and television if the children had their way)
- three Walkmans (which are used mostly on car journeys)
- a CD/tape player/radio in each of the children's bedrooms
- a radio in the kitchen (used around 8 a.m. and 6 p.m.)
- a CD player (which also has speakers in the kitchen)
- a colour television and VCR in the living room.

Like my situation, yours is probably not typical, in various ways. Three quarters of households have more than one television set, and the average household has 2.27 sets. 73% have access to teletext, 22% have digital stereo television sets, 20% have satellite dishes, 13% cable, about 28% a home computer, and 8% have access to the Internet (Independent Television Commission, 1999). Levels of ownership, and the huge growth of these over a mere seven years, is shown in Table 1.1.

TABLE 1.1 Home entertainment equipment in the home, per cent of all television viewers 1991 and 1998

	1991	1998
Video cassette recorder	72	85
Teletext	40	73
CD player	22	50
Personal computer	22	28
Video games	12	30
Satellite TV dish	8	20
Video camera	5	16
NICAM stereo television set	5	22
Cable television	3	13
Cable telephone	n/a	13
Wide screen television	n/a	6
Internet	n/a	8
Have none of these	20	4

n/a = not asked.
Source: *Television: The Public's View 1999*, pp.6–7

In short, there has been a massive increase of technology in the home in recent years. None of the goods listed in Table 1.1 shows a declining level of ownership. Most recently we have seen the growth of households with multiple television sets distributed around the home, DVD, and the growth of interactive services accessed by television, telephone line or cable. Increasingly our houses are places where we consume media from a growing diversity of sources and technologies, and for an increasing number of hours of the week.

3.2 Work

At work we have seen equally dramatic changes. In recent years production has been restructured in ways which are commonly characterized in terms of 'from Fordism to post-Fordism'. Fordism – a system, as you might guess, pioneered by the car manufacturer Henry Ford – is rooted in five principles:

- standardization of product (to enable the economies of mass, as opposed to craft, production)

- mechanization (which is enabled by standardizing processes)

- Taylorism, or scientific management (breaking down a task into its smallest components, and thus requiring skills of as low a level as possible)

- the separation of conception (thinking) from execution (doing), with engineers instructing a worker how to perform the task, preventing the changing of that task in any way, and a huge middle management to plan and monitor processes

- production lines (to regulate the pace of work).

The outcome was that the Ford Model T cost about a tenth of the cost of a craft-built car in the USA in 1916, and Ford took 50 per cent of the market. Fordism involved a high set-up cost (the machinery and line), a low unit (or marginal) cost, and a mass output and market. It is an approach which transformed a succession of factories and sectors during the course of the twentieth century, and is seen as characterizing industrialism and the modern era. Taylor and Ford were embraced around the world, notably by Lenin and the USSR's organization of planning and production, with its emphasis on scale and standardization.

Post-Fordism, by contrast, emerged in the closing decades of the twentieth century and, it is commonly claimed, characterizes the organization of production and society today. This is associated with flexibility, customization, niche markets, and just-in-time delivery – features sometimes associated with Japanese corporations and referred to as Japanization. Organizational functions which are not core to a business, such as cleaning or canteens, are sub-contracted out. Relationships of trust and flexibility are established with suppliers (replacing the contract culture of Fordism) so that, for example, immediate and reliable delivery is the primary requirement, and cost negotiated later. Production machinery has become more programmable and flexible. Stock levels have been reduced and quality has been improved by using workers' mental as well as manual labour. Continuous learning and change are embraced, while middle management has been reduced and its functions computerized. Some key characteristics of Fordism and post-Fordism are summarized in Table 1.2, which shows how both terms are ways of characterizing not just work but also society.

TABLE 1.2 Characteristics of Fordism and post-Fordism

	Fordism	Post-Fordism
Basis of economy	Industry	Information
Form of production	Mass production	Flexible specialization
Form of work organization	Bureaucracy	Flexibility
Core symbol	Factory	Computer
Service provision	In-house	Out-sourced
Workplace organization	Hierarchy	Team
Workforce organization	Unionized	Individual contract
Basis of economic transactions	Legal contract	Trust
Employment	One trade for life	Flexible/multi-skilled
Social organization	Collectivism	Individualism
Social division	Class	Lifestyle
Organization	Planning	Laissez-faire
Market	Mass	Niche

ACTIVITY 1.4

Think of an organization you know something about which has many features of the Fordist model. Note the ways it is Fordist. Then think of an organization of a more post-Fordist nature. Run through the characteristics listed above to see which apply, and note how.

COMMENT

Nearly all organizations and factories operate in more post-Fordist and less Fordist ways than in the past. Overall there has been a dramatic demise of Fordist features (the assembly line producing mass products), and a growth of post-Fordist features. At the same time, numerous Fordist features persist.

3.3 The military

Warfare has always involved the deployment of technology, but the rate at which military technology has been transformed in the past century is phenomenal. The cultural theorist Kevin Robins and sociologist Frank Webster explain how the First World War brought about the 'industrialisation of war', which lasted until the 1970s (Robins and Webster, 1999). Crucially, this involved the close harnessing of industrial production (and science) to serve warfare. In both world wars, the entire population was mobilized for the war effort, all production was redirected to the war, huge numbers fought, and there was considerable state intervention (for example of transport and energy). More recently, they argue, industrial warfare has been replaced by what they call information warfare or cyber-warfare. Information has always been crucial in war, but today its volume has grown enormously and its strategic significance has increased. Information is gathered and processed regarding the enemy, the deployment of troops and other resources, and the management of public opinion back home. Information has permeated many dimensions of modern warfare, including surveillance satellites and 'smart' weapons. About one-third of the UK Ministry of Defence's equipment procurement budget, currently about £9 billion per annum, is for 'command and information systems' alone. An ever-increasing proportion of the budget is spent on technology rather than personnel. Warfare nowadays involves more rapid response, more professional and technological resources, more pre-programming and automation, and considerable perception management (to ensure continuing domestic support for the war). The Gulf War in 1991 involved meticulous handling of media coverage in what has been referred to as 'the most "communicated" event so far in human history' (Zolo, 1997, cited in Robins and Webster, 1999, p.157). Rather than mobilizing the entire population and economy for a war effort, information warfare relies on 'capturing only the leading edges of industrial innovation for military purposes – for instance, electronic engineering, computing, telecommunications and aerospace' (Robins and Webster, 1999, p.156).

Preparation for information warfare absorbs vast resources, it has diverted research and development from other possible priorities, and has shaped the core technologies we have today. The Ministry of Defence is British industry's single largest customer. It has been estimated that 12 per cent of UK manufacturing and 37 per cent of its engineering is dependent on military sales. Aerospace and electronics absorb over half of the annual defence procurement budget. In short, military priorities and developments lie at the heart of the information society. Military research has generated most civilian technologies, notably the integrated circuits and miniaturization which lie at the core of computer technology. More than this, information warfare has 'nurtured the growth of a culture of control and surveillance' (Robins and Webster, 1999, p.158).

3.4 The state and surveillance

This leads to our fourth area, how new technology has enabled an increase in the level of monitoring and surveillance of citizens and consumers by the state and commercial organizations. Our movement and lifestyle is increasingly monitored. Supermarkets compile databases of our food consumption, telephone companies monitor who we talk to, banks monitor our purchases and location, and other private organizations can access marketing databases which record our personal details, including county court judgements (used for credit rating) and postcodes, which represent important characteristics of our area. Never before have people been monitored so systematically and commodified to such an extent.

Credit rating companies hold your electoral roll entry, your repayment history (including any arrears or defaults on a credit agreement), county court judgements against you, and the credit history of related parties such as your family or others at your address. One problem is that many people do not know that such records exist, or how to check or correct them. Many of us are refused credit for various reasons, at various times in our life and most of us never know the reason why. Research on private credit reference databases suggests that one in ten of their records contain errors (Collinson, 2000) and, for some, the consequences can be serious in terms of the opportunities available.

ACTIVITY 1.5

If you would like a copy of your credit reference query file, write to Experian Customer Help Desk, PO Box 8000, Nottingham NG1 5GX or Eqinfax, Dept 1E, PO Box 3001, Glasgow G81 2DT, enclosing a cheque or postal order for £2.

COMMENT

There is a strong likelihood that you will learn nothing new, but some of you may be surprised. When I requested my record from one of these organizations I was sent details of credit at various organizations as well as county court judgements relating to both relatives who had long since left my address and to various neighbours.

Some people have found that they are constantly refused credit because, for instance, as non British citizens they are not on the electoral roll. If you have the same name as a previous occupant of your house, you may find yourself tarred with an unattractive credit history – a more common problem if you are called Jones, Patel or Smith. The same initials as an errant relative will pose the same problem. Others are the victim of inaccurate information, generated when credit paid off in time was incorrectly noted as unpaid. Incorrect records of fraud have been found, again leading to the refusal of credit.

The main concern for privacy, however, appears to come from the growth of surveillance by the state. Nation-states have always gathered data on their citizens but today, with ICTs, we are experiencing this on a scale which is unprecedented. Government records on us have multiplied enormously. They include births, marriages and deaths, health and social services, insurance, tax, DVLC's car and driving licence records, and police databases (some of which record 'intelligence' on citizens, as opposed to factual data relating to criminal activities). Added to this are video technologies which increasingly monitor public and private spaces.

Obviously, such databases enable people to claim and deliver services efficiently, and they contribute to order and security in public spaces. If we have done nothing wrong, what fears should we have of state databases, for example those held by the police? On the other hand, as well as sustaining state surveillance, the same ICTs offer possibilities for radical or alternative groups to organize, mobilize and communicate, from victims of oppressive regimes such as the Zapatistas to truckers concerned about fuel taxes.

ACTIVITY 1.6

Make a list of all the organizations or databases which you think hold information on you. Do you think any of these poses any threat to you?

Arguments about the democratizing possibilities of new ICTs have to be explored in the context of power, and ICTs offer tremendously enhanced capability to the powers of the state. New ICTs add several new features to state surveillance. First, is the *volume* of data. Never before has the state known so much about its citizens. Second, this can now be accessed remotely, and by a large number of officials. No longer does one have to enter the right building or filing cabinet to obtain access. Finally, with digital data, the information is cross-referenced as never before.

Jeremy Bentham, the social reformer and philosopher, developed a plan for a panoptic penitentiary in 1791. This was for a building which would accommodate prisoners in individual cells where they could be viewed by a guard, but the prisoners themselves could not view the guard (through the use of lighting and blinds) nor could they see one another. Control was to be exercised by prisoners sensing that they were under constant surveillance, with no privacy. Although no such prison was built, its principles have been influential. It can be argued that, with contemporary electronic surveillance, the Panopticon is reproduced, albeit freed of its physical constraints. In other words, the state can see and know much about what its citizens do. Crucially, as citizens we know this, and tailor our actions and thought accordingly. For instance, which of us wouldn't at least hesitate to sign a petition if, as a result, it is less likely that we got a good job in the future?

So across a breadth of social realms – and we have just explored the home, work, the military and surveillance – we can see some profoundly transformatory ways in which new technologies are being applied. In the next chapter we take this exploration a stage further and examine the work of Daniel Bell and Manuel Castells, the two social theorists who have laid the foundations of debates about the information society.

Theories of the information society

Hugh Mackay

chapter 2

1   INTRODUCTION

A diversity of social scientists have studied the information society or provided analyses of contemporary social and cultural transformations. Theorists of these transformations can be categorized in a number of ways. The first distinction is between those who foreground new *technology*, who see technological development as the catalyst for social change, and, on the other hand, those who focus more on political, economic, social or cultural factors which drive history. Many of the latter refer not to the information society, but to late modernity, post-industrialism, postmodernism or globalization to characterize the contemporary world and its transformation. Some writers focus on quantitative measures of change, while others root their arguments in more qualitative data. Frank Webster argues that the former may well identify increasing volumes of information, a larger information sector and the proliferation of ICTs, but pay less attention to the meaning or significance of such transformations (Webster, 1995). A further distinction is between the more utopian and the more pessimistic, with the debate remarkably polarized on this count. For some, the information society is a new era of greater freedom and fulfilment, with improved access to more information indicative of the enhanced freedom we enjoy. Others, however, point to the continuation of long-standing inequalities, or the exacerbation of these with new systems of exploitation, control and domination.

Probably the two best-known theorists of the information society are the American sociologist Daniel Bell and the urban theorist Manuel Castells. It is these two, more than any others, who have set up and shaped the contours of information society debates, so we shall deal with their ideas at some length.

2   BELL'S POST-INDUSTRIAL SOCIETY

'... far and away the best known characterisation of the "information society"' (Webster, 1995, p.30) is that of the American sociologist Daniel Bell. Bell wrote initially about 'post-industrial society' not 'information society', but in his later work he often refers to 'information society' by which he means the 'post-industrial society' – so the distinction matters little to him.

Bell's analysis of contemporary society rejected prevailing Marxist approaches which focused on class and the capitalist system of exploitation to explain social change. Instead, Bell argued that Western economies had de-industrialized, with a declining percentage of the workforce working in the manufacturing sector, and the growth of employment in the service sector. Table 2.1 shows clearly the transformation which lies at the heart of Bell's thesis.

Writing in 1974, Bell refers to a coming revolution in which the computer has a central role. He is describing a trajectory from pre-industrial, through industrial, to post-industrial societies, with predominant modes of employment shifting at each stage so that today we live in a service society. This can be illustrated by considering the decline of employment in coal (a primary, extractive, industry) and shipbuilding (a heavy manufacturing, secondary, industry), and the growth of employment in insurance and McDonald's fast food outlets. Bell refers to pre-industrial society as raw muscle power against nature; the industrial age as characterized by machinery; and post-industrial society based on services, when 'what counts is not raw muscle power, or energy, but information' (Bell, 1974, p.127). In 1970, 65 per cent of the US labour force was working in services, and less than 5 per cent in agriculture, which shows clearly that the shift to a service society had taken place in the USA. Bell acknowledges that there has always been a substantial service sector – servants in the nineteenth century, banking and transport, for example – but argues that in post-industrial society services are of an entirely different character. They encompass education, health and social services, but also systems analysis and design, and analysing and processing information. It is these latter categories that have grown enormously. The expansion of these jobs represents the burgeoning post-industrial society or (as he calls it in his later work) information society. Social scientists, however, have to treat such claims with caution.

Think carefully about this seemingly well-substantiated argument, that we have experienced de-industrialization and a growth of service and information work. Is it a plausible and coherent argument? What empirical evidence would prove or disprove Bell's thesis? Would the same evidence support other explanations?

TABLE 2.1   Four-sector aggregation of the US labour force

Year	Information sector	Agriculture sector	Industry sector	Service sector	Total
		Experienced civilian workforce			
1860	480,604	3,364,230	3,065,024	1,375,525	8,286,283
1870	601,018	5,884,971	4,006,789	2,028,438	12,521,216
1880	1,131,415	7,606,590	4,386,409	4,281,970	17,406,384
1890	2,821,500	8,464,500	6,393,883	5,074,149	22,754,032
1900	3,732,371	10,293,179	7,814,652	7,318,947	29,159,149
1910	5,930,193	12,377,785	14,447,382	7,044,592	39,799,952
1920	8,016,054	14,718,742	14,492,300	8,061,342	45,288,438
1930	12,508,959	10,415,623	18,023,113	10,109,284	51,056,979
1940	13,337,958	8,233,624	19,928,422	12,082,376	53,582,380
1950	17,815,978	6,883,446	22,154,285	10,990,378	57,844,087
1960	28,478,317	4,068,511	23,597,364	11,661,326	67,805,518
1970	37,167,513	2,466,883	22,925,095	17,511,639	80,071,130
1980[1]	44,650,721	2,012,157	21,558,824	27,595,297	95,816,999
Percentages					
1860	5.8	40.6	37.0	16.6	100
1870	4.8	47.0	32.0	16.2	100
1880	6.5	43.7	25.2	24.6	100
1890	12.4	37.2	28.1	22.3	100
1900	12.8	35.3	26.8	25.1	100
1910	14.9	31.1	36.3	17.7	100
1920	17.7	32.5	32.0	17.8	100
1930	24.5	20.4	35.3	19.8	100
1940	24.9	15.4	37.2	22.5	100
1950	30.8	11.9	38.3	19.0	100
1960	42.0	6.0	34.8	17.2	100
1970	46.4	3.1	28.6	21.9	100
1980[1]	46.6	2.1	22.5	28.8	100

[1]Bureau of Labour Statistics projection.
Source: Bell, 1980, p.522

Clearly, IT and telecommunication work has increased enormously. They are areas of the economy and employment largely unheard of until recent decades and they are now central. But, because they are of such a large scale and significance, it does not mean that Bell's argument is the only one supported by the evidence. Is it the case that, in the same way as the primary sector was overtaken by the secondary sector, the secondary sector is now being eclipsed by the tertiary?

Gershuny and Miles (1983) have criticized this notion of the 'march through the sectors' on a number of counts. They point to the growth which has taken place in manufacturing in the so-called service-based economies of the information age. Rather than a shift from manufacturing employment, a better explanation of the data is a shift from agriculture to service employment. Between 1840 and 1980 the proportion of the workforce of the UK employed in manufacturing remained at around 45 to 50 per cent; its collapse after 1980 was a consequence of global recession and monetarist economic policies, rather than some other dynamic which led to the growth of the service sector. As Frank Webster points out, 'other than in Britain, nowhere has a majority of the population at any time worked in industry' (Webster, 1995, p.41). This encourages caution regarding the links which Bell makes in his argument.

Bell's argument, however, is not simply about the transition to a service economy. For Bell, the post-industrial society is characterized by the centrality of scientific knowledge, and by scientific knowledge directing social change. Bell accepts readily that every society has used scientific knowledge, but argues that never before has science driven history as it does today. The nineteenth-century inventors such as Graham Bell (the telephone) or Thomas Edison (electricity) were essentially tinkerers, he writes, working by trial-and-error combined with brilliant intuition, rather than focusing on scientific equations.

Think of an occupation or industry with which you are familiar. In relation to this specific case, do you think that scientific knowledge occupies a greater significance today than before? Are other explanations possible for the changes which have taken place? More generally, what data, or evidence, would support or disprove Bell's argument about scientific knowledge?

Bell uses no empirical data of his own but draws on the work of a number of economists, notably Fritz Machlup and Marc Porat – work which, incidentally, the information theorist Alistair Duff, who is sympathetic to Bell's thesis, refers to as 'riddled with ambiguities and errors' (Duff, 1998, p.382). Machlup found that between 1947 and 1958 the knowledge industries expanded at a compound growth rate of 10.6 per cent per annum. Bell acknowledges that Machlup's definition of knowledge was 'somewhat unsatisfactory', based as it was on subjective interpretation rather than any objective measure of what has to be known to perform a job.

What difficulties can you see in measuring knowledge production, processing and distribution in the economy? In broad terms, how would you go about this? What are the limitations of your approach?

These are large and complex questions. First, you would have to define each of these three types of knowledge work, and define 'knowledge' itself. Machlup grouped 30 industries into five classes of knowledge production, processing and distribution: education; research and development; communication media; information machines; and information services. In some senses the classification seems clear, or obvious: a teacher's work is very much rooted in their knowledge of their subject and of ways of teaching and learning. But does having, for instance, *more* doctors (an information occupation) mean that we live in an information society, or merely one which provides better health care? Does a central heating engineer work with more codified or scientific knowledge than the more humbly termed plumber? Such questions are enormously complex and fraught with difficulty – separating out the 'knowledge' component of every job, and doing this longitudinally (i.e. over time). Although one measure of 'knowledge' might be 'length of time in training', this ignores background knowledge (e.g. compulsory GCSE mathematics), and fails to separate skill (practical doing) from knowledge. Given the absence of any agreed method of making such measurement and categorization, let alone the availability of suitable data, this is a considerable research task.

Bell acknowledges some of these difficulties. He argues that to identify the scope of the information economy one needs a set of categories which includes knowledge (e.g. doctors or lawyers), entertainment (e.g. television or music industries), economic transactions (e.g. banking or insurance), and infrastructure services (e.g. telecommunications). In the absence of his own data on this set of categories, Bell turns to the work of Marc Porat, who examined the proportion of economic activity which can be attributed to information activities. Porat identified gross national product (GNP) and income data to define a primary sector which sells information services to consumers (e.g. banking or advertising) and a secondary sector which is involved in planning and information activities. Without going into the detail involved in such a study, Porat's conclusion was that nearly 50 per cent of GNP and more than 50 per cent of wages and salaries in the USA in 1967 derived from the production, processing and distribution of information goods and services (as shown in Figure 2.1).

This fits the common-sense understanding that we have witnessed the rise of various sectors and occupations and the demise of others during the course of the twentieth century. Crucial to Porat's and Bell's research and argument, however, are the notions of 'information' and 'knowledge'. As we have explained, Bell talks of a 'march through the sectors', of declining agriculture and extractive work, the rise of manufacturing and now its decline

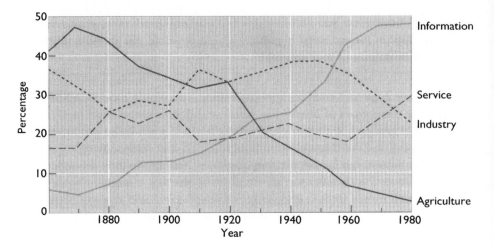

FIGURE 2.1   Four-sector aggregation of the US workforce, 1860–1980
Source: Bureau of Labour Statistics, cited in Bell, 1980, p.521

in the process known as 'de-industrialization', and finally the rise of the service sector. To this 'service sector' Bell, like Porat, adds an 'information sector'. For Bell, information and knowledge are the 'crucial variables' of the post-industrial economy. By information he is referring to the storage, retrieval and processing of data, which has become the essential resource in society.

To argue that there has been a growth of the information sector, however, is rather different from the fairly incontrovertible growth of the service sector. What is the relationship between the service sector and the information sector? Bell does not really define what he means by a 'service', only contrasting it with the 'goods' of industrial society. Can we distinguish service *work* (as opposed to a service sector) in a way which might be meaningful? Cleaning, transport and accountancy can all be classified as 'services' (and might be if these services are delivered by cleaning, transport or accountancy firms). Such services, however, when delivered 'in-house' in manufacturing organizations would be classified as manufacturing jobs. For example, a van driver at a steel company would be classified as working in 'manufacturing', but if the steel company contracted out its transport, the same job would be in the tertiary sector. Similarly, the carpenter at McDonald's is a service worker. In other words, the easy divisions of service and manufacturing are unreliable, if not meaningless. As Webster concludes, 'a good deal of service work is engaged, not in consuming the wealth created by industry, but in assisting in its production' (Webster, 1995, p.43). Much service work, for example transport, finance and insurance, would not function without the manufacturing economy.

Whatever the problems with his analysis of occupations and sectors, Bell's writing demonstrates an impressive breadth of vision, particularly given the date of his writing. Linking the 'information explosion' with both scientific knowledge and new technology, he discusses the growing demand for news and entertainment:

> The information explosion is a set of reciprocal relations between the expansion of science, the hitching of that science to a new technology, and the growing demand for news, entertainment and instrumental knowledge, all in the context of a rapidly increasing population, more literate and more educated, living in a vastly enlarged world that is now tied together, almost in real time, by cable, telephone and international satellite, whose inhabitants are made aware of each other by the vivid pictorial imagery of television, and that has at its disposal large data banks of computerized information.
>
> (Bell, 1980, pp.525–6)

Thus Bell acknowledges the crucial role of television, though fails to develop its significance – he nowhere charts or quantifies the mass media, or media flows, nor does he discuss their cultural significance.

We have already challenged Bell's conception of changes in sectors of economic activity and shifts to a knowledge-based economy. But how do we evaluate his definition and use of the notion of knowledge? By 'knowledge', Bell means the organized set of statements of facts or ideas which present a researched judgement or an experimental result which is transmitted systematically to others. This seems a useful definition, and it seems irrefutable that we have seen the dramatic growth of such codified knowledge, and that production and organization have become more dependent on it – in some senses this is an analysis which follows Max Weber's work on rationality. For Bell, if knowledge is involved systematically in the transformation of resources then knowledge, not labour, is the source of value. Knowledge has replaced labour as the source of added value in the national product 'just as capital and labour have been the central variables of industrial society, so information and knowledge are the crucial variables in post-industrial society' (Bell, 1980, p.506). In some ways this seems a plausible argument: increasingly, firms regard the skills of their workforce as their greatest asset, and many politicians argue that we need work and an economy which is based on high added value as an alternative to cheap, unskilled work. Nonetheless, at this point Bell's argument seems somewhat problematic: an increasing dependence of production on knowledge does not mean a reduced importance of labour. 'Intelligent machines' still have to be developed, maintained, upgraded and operated. They will displace much work, de-skill much of what remains, but also increase the value and strategic significance of the labour that remains, and the labour which is involved in its operation and development. In other words, the relationship of knowledge to social change seems more complex than Bell suggests, and its growth is perhaps less transformatory of social relations than he argues. Thus we can identify a lack of coherence in his argument.

Another point at which it is easy to part company with Bell is when his values become more overt, which happens in his visions of the future. By and large, social scientists are concerned with explaining the social, with developing theories and concepts which help us to understand social interaction and social transformation. Rarely does a social scientist make claims which would enjoy the status of a scientific law. Rarely, too, do social scientists play the role of foretelling the future, though their work, to varying degrees, commonly allows some extrapolation or speculation. Bell, however, is something of an exception, in that he devotes considerable attention in his work to his vision of the future. He moves from data and analysis to prognostication, and even prescription, saying what *should be*, by addressing the implications of his analysis for governments, policies and economies.

More than this, Bell argues that the changes underway are a good thing. Again, it is unusual for social scientists to be as explicit about their value preferences in such a way. He refers to the 'overflowing of all the world's traditions of art, music and literature into a new, universal container, accessible to all and obligatory upon all' (Bell, 1974, p.188). He argues that the rise of professional work means not only more information in circulation, but also profound qualitative social change. Professionals are oriented towards their clients, and thus society transforms into a *caring* society: in post-industrial society people are no longer the cogs in the wheels of industrial capitalism, but benefit from the person-oriented focus of professionals, leading to a 'new consciousness' and a 'communal society' (Bell, 1974, p.220). According to Bell, notions of public interest, the environment, the care of the elderly and education become more important than more restricted concerns of maximizing the return on capital. He even argues that poorer countries can 'leapfrog' the industrial age and transform their economies directly from a primary to a tertiary basis. Retrospectively, all this seems remarkably optimistic for a writer in the 1970s. You can judge for yourself whether he was right!

SUMMARY

- Daniel Bell is a leading theorist of the information society. He focuses in particular on the rise of the service or information sector or economy.

- His work is characterized by claims which are not always supported by the evidence he cites.

- His values intrude upon his analysis of trends, and extrapolations from these.

- His evidence, in places, is lacking in validity.

- We have identified inconsistencies in his arguments, where claims made are not the only, or even best, way of explaining the evidence he cites.

3 TECHNOLOGICAL DETERMINISM

Underlying Bell's work is a very clear technological determinism. He sees technology as the basis of enhanced productivity, and productivity as having transformed the economy. Technology is central to his argument, whilst the common social science categories – class, capital and power, for example – are largely absent from his work. In this sense, Bell's work epitomizes the information society literature, as Webster argues:

> So much commentary on the 'information age' starts from a naive and taken-for-granted position: 'there has been an "information technology revolution", this will have and is having profound social consequences, here are the sorts of *impacts* one may anticipate and which may already have been evidenced'. This sets out with such a self-evidently firm sense of direction, and it follows such a neat linear logic – technological innovation results in social change – that it is almost a pity to announce that it is simply the wrong point of departure for those embarking on a journey to see where informational trends, technological and other, are leading. At the least, recognition of the contribution of social theory moves one away from the technological determinism which tends to dominate a great deal of consideration of the issues ...

(Webster, 1995, p.215)

Technological determinism is probably the most common way in which the relationship between technology and society is conceived, though one might not expect a social scientist to take this perspective. By technological determinism is meant the notion that technology shapes society, that technology is an independent factor, somehow *outside* society, and that technical change *causes* and is responsible for social change. In its stronger variants it asserts that technology is the *main* determinant of social change, the prime mover in history; whilst weaker forms of technological determinism see technology as one among other factors which shape history. 'Harder' forms of technological determinism argue that a given technology *will lead to* particular outcomes; whilst 'softer' forms see a given technology as *enabling* or *facilitating* potentials or opportunities, as Lynn White puts it, 'a new device merely opens a door; it does not compel one to enter' (White, 1978, p.28). Both share a view that technological development represents the unfolding of the scientific laws of nature which drive social progress.

Studies of science and of the work of scientists, however, show a rather different picture – of science being shaped by the society in which it is undertaken. Research shows that the direction and rate of scientific work is shaped clearly by social priorities; that models, concepts, metaphors and images prevailing in a society have shaped the direction of work and the interpretations of scientists; and even that 'proof' and 'facts' are social processes (Shapin, 1982; Barnes and Edge, 1982). So science, rather than some neutral or asocial activity, is itself profoundly social.

An example of technological determinism is the argument that computer technology causes unemployment. The reality is that the effects of technology are not built in to the technology, that they are not determined. Rather, they vary according to the social context. In some situations, introducing IT enhances competitiveness and leads to a growth in the number of jobs, not unemployment.

Technological determinism is important both because of its prevalence *and* because it leaves us feeling passive about technology. If technological change is going to happen anyway, then there's not much point in worrying about it, and there's not much we can do about it. So it has led many – including some social scientists – to focus on the *effects* of technology, and perhaps on how to control the worst excesses of the latest development or on how society can *adapt* to the constant stream of new technologies.

Many social scientists approach this rather differently. What they have tended to address is not how societies could, or do, adapt to new technologies, but how particular social factors give rise to particular technologies. In other words, the relationship of technology to society is not simply one of effects; technologies are social in their *origins*, too. Most obviously, they are the outcome of complex social processes – commonly to achieve clear military or commercial ends – rather than of any neutral or disinterested research and development, usable for good or ill, depending on social priorities. Langdon Winner, a researcher in technology and society, refers to two ways in which technologies can be inherently political. First, they can be designed, consciously or unconsciously, to open certain options and to close others. The example he uses is the New York developer and road builder from the 1930s to the 1970s, Robert Moses, who (Winner claims) designed a road system to access Jones Beach which would in effect exclude poorer, black, people from using the beach.

> Anyone who has travelled the highways of America and has become used to the normal height of overpasses may well find something a little odd about some of the bridges over the parkways on Long Island, New York. Many of the overpasses are extraordinarily low, having as little as nine feet of clearance at the curb. Even those who happened to notice this structural peculiarity would not be inclined to attach any special meaning to it. In our accustomed way of looking at things like roads and bridges we see the details of form as innocuous, and seldom give them a second thought.
>
> It turns out, however, that the two hundred or so low-hanging overpasses on Long Island were deliberately designed to achieve a particular social effect. Robert Moses, the master builder of roads, parks, bridges, and other public works from the 1920s to the 1970s in New York, had these overpasses built to specifications that would discourage the presence of buses on his parkways. According to

evidence provided by Robert A. Caro in his biography of Moses, the reasons reflect Moses' social-class bias and racial prejudice. Automobile-owning whites of 'upper' and 'comfortable middle' classes, as he called them, would be free to use the parkways for recreation and commuting. Poor people and blacks, who normally used public transit, were kept off the roads because the twelve-foot tall buses could not get through the overpasses. One consequence was to limit access of racial minorities and low-income groups to Jones Beach, Moses' widely acclaimed public park. Moses made doubly sure of this result by vetoing a proposed extension of the Long Island Railroad to Jones Beach.

As a story in recent American political history, Robert Moses' life is fascinating. His dealings with mayors, governors, and presidents, and his careful manipulation of legislatures, banks, labour unions, the press and public opinion are all matters that political scientists could study for years. But the most important and enduring results of his work are his technologies, the vast engineering projects that give New York much of its present form. For generations after Moses has gone and the alliances he forged have fallen apart, his public works, especially the highways and bridges he built to favour the use of the automobile over the development of mass transit, will continue to shape that city. Many of his monumental structures of concrete and steel embody a systematic social inequality, a way of engineering relationships among people that, after a time, becomes just another part of the landscape. As planner Lee Koppleman told Caro about the low bridges on Wantagh Parkway, 'The old son-of-gun had made sure that buses would *never* be able to use his goddamned parkways'.

(MacKenzie and Wajcman, 1995, pp.28–9)

Second, Winner argues that some technologies *require* or are more compatible with some social relations than with others. In the former category, he argues that nuclear power plants *require* the techno–scientific–military–industrial complex, they can't exist without it; whereas, he argues, solar power is more compatible with decentralized institutions. Thus Winner explores one way – in his terms, a political way – in which technologies are shaped.

A more concrete example of social shaping, albeit of a domestic technology rather than an information technology, is a fascinating research project reported by the sociologist of technology Ruth Schwartz Cowan (1995). Reflecting on why electric refrigerators became the dominant form of fridge in the home, even though the alternative gas technology involves no moving parts and so less wear and tear, Cowan looked at the social and not technological terms of development. She found that to understand why we all have refrigerators which hum we have to look not at the technical characteristics of the two types, but the social circumstances surrounding their development. In the 1920s numerous companies were working on refrigerators because the prospects of large profits were good, given the number of households which looked likely to appreciate (and were able to afford) the technology. General Electric engaged in massive, unusual and highly prominent advertising and public relations. Manufacturers of gas refrigerators, on the other hand, lacked the necessary capital to develop and market their product. Cowan concludes that: 'The demise of the gas refrigerator was not the result of inherent deficiencies in the machine itself. ... The latter succeeded for reasons that were as much social and economic as technical; its development was encouraged by a few companies that could draw upon vast technical and financial resources' (Cowan, 1995, pp.213–14).

Sociologists of technology, unlike Bell, have sought to explore the ways in which social forces have shaped our technology, as opposed to the orthodoxy of technological determinism, which sees technological development as unproblematic, asocial, and determining of social arrangements. Acknowledging that technology is socially shaped does not, of course, mean that technologies have *no* effects – so we must be careful here not to throw the baby out with the bath-water. Attributing some degree of determination to technology seems useful: how could we make sense of the contemporary era without taking account of the capabilities and limitations of our prevailing technology? Would anyone want to deny the effects of the Internet on the traditional media or economy?

Bell, writing in 1974, said that computers have had comparatively little effect on individuals' lives, and even that the telephone, *lifts* and television had wreaked greater social change than the main technologies of the past 25 years (Bell, 1974, p.318). So, interestingly, although he saw modern computing as changing society, and able to achieve an ordered mass society, what he had in mind was mainframe computers. This is technological determinism, but regarding a technology hardly mentioned today. The main point, however, is that he fails to acknowledge or explore the social shaping of technology. Rather, he views technology as profoundly determining, even though he had in mind some technologies which today are not seen as particularly significant.

SUMMARY

Technological determinism:

- is the most common way of conceiving of the technology–society relationship
- accords primacy to the technological
- takes various forms (hard and soft)
- leads to a focus on effects, and a passivity towards technology
- is rejected by social scientists who, instead, point to ways in which technologies are socially shaped.

4   CASTELLS' 'NETWORK SOCIETY'

Manuel Castells is Professor of Sociology and Planning at the University of California, Berkeley, and is the leading theorist of the network society. The sociologist Anthony Giddens describes Castells' recent work as 'perhaps the most significant attempt that anyone has yet written to come to terms with the extraordinary transformations now going on in the social world' (Castells, 1996, back cover). Castells is the author of a recent trilogy, which totals over 1,200 pages, entitled *The Information Age* (Castells, 1996, 1997, 1998). He has appeared on the BBC programme *Newsnight* and suchlike, has become a well-known sociologist of the information society, and has been described as 'the first great philosopher of cyberspace'. In this section we'll examine the essence of his argument at some length.

Castells' analysis is based on the outcome of the combination of technological innovation, capitalist restructuring and the search for identity. Between them, these forces are transforming society, and especially its cities and regions. In developing his argument Castells examines the global economy, the nature of organizations in the informational economy, the transformation of work, national and ethnic identities, social movements, feminism, the family and sexuality, the state, democracy and politics, the collapse of the USSR, social exclusion, the global criminal economy, the reunification of Europe, and the rise of the Pacific region. It's a formidable and far-reaching œuvre. It draws mainly on quantitative data, mostly from others' research or official bodies. The core of his argument, however, is not hard to summarize or to grasp. It is rooted in a set of debates which are well-rehearsed in the social sciences today: about social polarization; surveillance; the growing focus on lifestyles, consumption and identities; the breakdown of old patterns and associations; and the restructuring of work. The originality of Castells' contribution lies in his synthesis of this enormous diversity, his global focus, and the core concepts he develops.

Castells' argument – unlike that of some other information society theorists – is *not* that we have moved on from capitalism. Rather, it is that the 'network society' represents a *new variant of capitalism*, and the basis of its recovery from the crisis of the 1970s. Unlike Bell, Castells sees growing inequality, exclusion and polarization with the demise of labour-intensive industries and their replacement with production flexibility.

Castells distinguishes between the 'mode of development' and the 'mode of production'. The latter is a well-established Marxist concept relating to the organization of economic production: under capitalism, production is organized for the profit of the owners of capital, and workers are able to sell only their labour. Castells argues that, with the rise of the *informational mode of development*, we are witnessing the emergence of a new socio-economic paradigm, one with information processing at its core. Different societies, he argues, have different modes of development. Modes of development evolve according to their own logic, they can be seen as the technical way of achieving particular social arrangements or a particular mode of production. Castells is clear to distance himself from the 'information technology revolution' paradigm of the 1970s, arguing that this technological revolution didn't *create* the network society, though was necessary to achieve this. Nonetheless, the network society is characterized by the centrality of information and IT. He also distinguishes his *informational* society from notions of the *information* society: the latter emphasizes the role of information in society but, Castells argues, information has always been critical in society. 'Informational', by contrast, indicates the 'specific form of social organisation in which information generation, processing and transmission become the fundamental sources of productivity and power, because of the technological conditions' (Castells, 1996, p.21). He says that this distinction is comparable with that between industry and industrial – an industrial society is not just one having industry, but is one permeated throughout by industrial organization.

In the informational economy, dominant functions and processes are increasingly organized around networks, which constitute a new social morphology. Organizations shift from bureaucracies to become *network enterprises* focusing on managing and responding to information flows. Successful organizations are those that are adaptable and flexible.

> ... the network enterprise is the specific set of linkages between different firms or segments, organised *ad hoc* for a specific project, and dissolving/reforming after the task is completed, e.g. IBM, Siemens, Toshiba. This ephemeral unit, The Project, around which a network of partners is built, is the actual operating unit of our economy, the one that generates profits or losses, the one that receives rewards and goes bust, and the one that hires and lays off, via its member organisations.

(Castells, 1999, p.401)

Economic activity becomes spatially dispersed but globally integrated in ways which generally reduce the significance of place but which enhance the strategic role of major cities. Castells proposes the hypothesis that the network society, the dominant social structure in the information age, is 'organised around new forms of time and space: timeless time, the space of flows' (Castells, 1999, p.405). By 'timeless time' he means 'the use of new information/communication technology in a relentless effort to annihilate time, to compress years in seconds, seconds in split seconds' (Castells, 1999, p.405). So this is an exacerbation and speed-up of a long-running tendency. He is clear that most people in the world still work and live by biological time and clock time, but he argues that *dominant* functions and social groups work with timeless time.

Places continue to be the focus of everyday life and of social and political control, they root culture and transmit history. But overlaying and dominating places are *flows* and Castells argues that, although these involve resistance to domination, 'the power of flows in the networks prevails over the flows of power' (Castells, 1999, p.409). He refers to the dependency of capitalists on 'uncontrollable' financial flows, implying something like the runaway and disordered world characterized by postmodern theorists (e.g. Jameson, 1991). His analysis is also congruent with what contemporary social sociologists often refer to as the 'cultural turn' when he refers to the breakdown of shared collective identities of class, nation and religion, and the rise of new social movements which are organized around identity. He refers to political power shifting from the nation-state and democratic systems to the media and other producers of culture. His analysis highlights fluidity: in the network society, social development cannot be shaped by specific social interests but emerges from the interconnectedness of different interests in networks.

Castells describes his networks as composed of *interconnected nodes* – places where information doesn't merely flow, but is collated, analysed and acted on. The major global corporations and banks are based in New York, Tokyo, London and Paris, and with them a managerial class with a cosmopolitan lifestyle. Members of this class are characterized by contacts around the world, extensive air travel, exotic restaurants and a high income used in part to buy services from the growing underclass which, by contrast, rarely leaves its physical neighbourhood. In contrast with earlier time–space arrangements, *flows have no distance between nodes* on the same network. In other words, geographical distance is irrelevant to connection and communication. The nature of a node depends on the type of network, but Castells provides some examples which indicate the truly global nature of his analysis: stock exchanges in the network of global finance flows; national councils of ministers and European Commissioners in the network that governs the EU; coca fields, clandestine laboratories and secret landing strips in the network of drug traffic; and television systems, entertainment studios, computer graphics milieu, news teams and mobile devices in the global culture network. These networks have become the basis of time–space ordering. The *network of flows* is crucial to domination and change in society: interconnected, global, capitalist networks organize economic activity using technology and information, and are the main source of power in society.

At the outset, Castells is critical of technological determinism: 'the dilemma of technological determinism is probably a false problem since technology *is* society, and society cannot be understood or represented without its technological tools' (Castells, 1996, p.5). At the same time, and like Bell, technology is something of a driving force in his analysis.

For Castells, contemporary technological innovation represents a fundamental change in how we see and experience the world. He reviews the historical impact of the invention of the alphabet, and asserts:

A technological transformation of similar historic dimension is taking place 2,700 years later. Namely the integration of various modes of communication into an interactive network. Or, in other words, the formation of a Super-text and Meta-language that, for the first time in history, integrates into the same system the written, oral, and audio-visual modalities of human communication. The human spirit reunites its dimensions in a new interaction between the two sides of the brain, machine, and social contexts.

(Castells, 1996, p.328)

The Internet and computer-mediated communication offer to transform the fabric of culture. Unlike the pessimism of those who point to the onward, repressive development of capitalism, the increasing commodification of culture, and growing surveillance and manipulation, Castells sees in the new communication medium new, democratic, possibilities for communication and participation. It limits the capacity of the dominant ideology to dominate. Instead, individuals can construct their own virtual worlds, which constitutes a democratization of images and beliefs.

Thus Castells links his argument to social movements. With globalization, the state is no longer the focus of political struggle, lacking the capacity to suppress or fulfil the demands of new social movements. These are characterized by communal resistance and the two broadly based movements of environmentalization and feminism. A 'new power system' has emerged, one characterized by 'the plurality of sources of authority' (Castells, 1997, p.303).

Like Bell, Castells concludes his work on an optimistic note. In his 'finale' he writes:

The dream of the Enlightenment, that reason and science would solve the problems of humankind, is within reach. Yet there is an extraordinary gap between our technological overdevelopment and our social underdevelopment. Our economy, society, and culture are built on interests, values, institutions and systems of representation that, by and large, limit collective creativity, confiscate the harvest of information technology, and deviate our energy into self-destructive confrontation. ... If people are informed, active, and communicate throughout the world; if business assumes its social responsibility; if the media become the messengers, rather than the message; if political actors react against cynicism, and restore belief in democracy; if culture is reconstructed from experience; if humankind feels the solidarity of the species throughout the globe; if we assert intergenerational solidarity by living in harmony with nature; if we depart from the exploration of our inner self, having made peace amongst ourselves. If all this is made possible by our informed, conscious, shared decision, while there is still time, maybe then, we may, at last, be able to live and let live, love and be loved.

(Castells, 1998, pp.359–60)

To begin to evaluate his work we need to know about his method. Castells (1996, p.25) states that 'This is not a book about books' and writes that he is not concerned with theories of the information society, post-industrialism or postmodernism. He proceeds to detail the sources of his data:

> while using a significant amount of statistical sources and empirical studies, I have tried to minimise the processing of data, to simplify an already excessively cumbersome book. Therefore, I tend to use data sources that find broad, accepted consensus among social scientists (for example, OECD, United Nations, World Bank, governments' official statistics, authoritative research monographs, generally reliable academic or business sources), except where such sources seem to be erroneous (such as Soviet GNP statistics or the World Bank's report on adjustment policies in Africa). I am aware of limitations in lending credibility to information that may not always be accurate, yet the reader will realise that there are numerous precautions taken in this text, so as to form conclusions usually on the basis of convergent trends from several sources, according to a methodology of triangulation with a well-established, successful tradition among historians, policemen and investigative reporters. Furthermore, the data, observations, and references presented in this book do not really aim at demonstrating but at suggesting hypotheses while constraining the ideas within a corpus of observation, admittedly selected with my research questions in mind but certainly not organised around preconceived answers. The methodology followed in this book, whose specific implications will be discussed in each chapter, is at the service of the overarching purpose of its intellectual endeavour: to propose some elements of an exploratory, cross-cultural theory of economy and society in the information age, *as it specifically refers to the emergence of a new social structure*. The broad scope of my analysis is required by the pervasiveness of the object of such analysis (informationalism) throughout the social domains and cultural expressions.
>
> (Castells, 1996, pp.26–7)

In passing, he occasionally refers to his own observations and experience. The nature of the observations is left rather unspecified, and the experience is, in several instances, of the student and worker demonstrations in Paris in 1968. Quite often he uses such phrases as 'following my scanning of the world' (Castells, 1998, p.352). He is quite explicit in stating his commitments and the significance of these for his research:

> I come from a time and a tradition, the political left of the industrial era, obsessed by the inscription on Marx's tomb at Highgate, his (and Engel's) eleventh thesis on Feuerbach. Transformative action was the ultimate goal of a truly meaningful intellectual endeavour. ... I do hope that this book, by raising some questions and providing empirical and theoretical elements to treat them, may contribute to informed social action in the pursuit of social change. In this case, I am not, and I do not want to be, a neutral, detached observer of the human drama.
>
> However, I have seen so much misled sacrifice, so many dead ends induced by ideology and such horrors provoked by artificial paradises of dogmatic politics that I want to convey a salutary reaction against trying to frame political practice in accordance with social theory, or, for that matter, with ideology. Theory and

research ... should be considered as a means of understanding our world, and should be judged exclusively on their accuracy, rigor and relevance. How these tools are used, and for what purpose, should be the exclusive prerogative of social actors themselves, in specific social contexts, and on behalf of their values and interests. ... The most fundamental political liberation is for people to free themselves from uncritical adherence to theoretical or ideological schemes, to construct their practice on the basis of their experience, while using whatever information or analysis is available to them, from a variety of sources.

(Castells, 1998, pp.358–9)

Turning to the links between data, theory and values in Castells' explanation, we can see that his work is both value laden and theoretically informed, in significant part by his roots in the French structural Marxism of Louis Althusser. (This focuses on how the bourgeois class and its capitalist state exercise power through the ideological state apparatuses, such as religion, the family, the media and the education system.) Notwithstanding Castells' opening comments (cited above), there would seem a strong case that his work is driven in a significant way by his theory. There is an interesting tension in that he describes the potential for liberation through the power of identity, but consistently deploys quantitative data to demonstrate the power of global capital and, behind that, of IT. In spite of this, he reflects on his analysis and is explicit about where he comes from and his commitments.

ACTIVITY 2.1

Try to answer the following questions about Castells' work.

- How does Castells account for his methods? (We have cited all that he says about his methods.)
- What are the implications of his values for his social science?

COMMENT

At the outset it's important to state that, by the standards of social science, Castells provides a cavalier and limited account of his methods. He draws on others' data, notably that which is 'generally reliable', except where sources 'seem to be erroneous'. However, he does not explain how he identifies reliability or error. That some of it may be incorrect doesn't matter too much, Castells writes, because he employs 'triangulation' (a technique he attributes to the police, amongst others), which is drawing comparable data from an additional source. He argues that, anyway, the data do not aim to 'demonstrate', but to 'suggest hypotheses'. This is interesting: it shows a link between data and explanation, indeed it suggests that the former gives rise to the latter. The methodology, he argues, is designed to serve his broad, overarching, cross-cultural intellectual endeavour – a theory of economy and society.

How would you begin to evaluate Castells' work?

In Chapter 3 we shall explore how social scientists evaluate social research in some detail. At this stage we shall confine ourselves to some general comments. First, many of Castells' data support the notion that the economy is globalized and is based on the transmission of information in financial markets. But this does not necessarily mean that the informational economy has superseded earlier forms of economic activity. Clearly, information is important to the operation of global finance markets, but such information is in many ways only a reflection of manufacturing and service performance in the economy: does the growth of information mean we have an informational economy? This is a question of *validity*.

Second, based as it is on mainly official statistics, Castells' data – with the caveats one would want to make about official statistics – seems largely *reliable*. By and large, subsequent data are likely to confirm those which he uses.

Third, Castells makes very broad, far-reaching claims which should apply to all of the cases to which the argument refers. To counter his arguments about the decline of the nation-state, one might point to their continuation and the continuation of national identities in the modern world, despite processes of globalization. New media can sustain traditional religions, as with tele-evangelism in the USA, rather than signal the arrival of a different culture and set of values. His argument may well be more applicable to the major cities of New York, Tokyo, London and Paris than to other places. This is a question of *comprehensiveness*.

The core of his argument, his thesis, is that we are moving towards a network society, characterized by information flows along networks between nodes. He gives examples of networks, flows and nodes, but these are neither quantified in any way nor described at all comprehensively. In other words, the detailed data he cites, though interesting, have only a tenuous link with his core argument. In this sense his work can be criticized for its lack of *coherence*. The lines of inference which run between data and concepts – known as construct validity – are weak. One can't help but wonder whether the theory came before the data or, to sound less sceptical, to wonder about the precise relationship between the data and his analysis. Castells assumes that data suggest explanation, but this raises the tension between theory and evidence. It appears that he lets theory drive argument, to a relatively high degree.

We can point to a lack of coherence in other ways. Some of these point to the plausibility and accuracy of his hidden assumptions, which is one aspect of coherence. How tenable is it, for example, to argue (following a Marxist model) that the network society is a form of capitalist society which is determined not (according to classical Marxism) by tensions between the forces and mode of production (between classes and how the economy is organized) but by the 'informational mode of development'? On what basis can we say that a society at any point in time is characterized by a particular mode of development? If the mode of development evolves according to its own logic, what drives history? Isn't this (like Bell) a form of technological determinism? More than this, isn't Castells reducing everything to networks, and then attributing enormous powers of determination to those networks? How can power reside in networks without reference to any other economic or material basis?

Finally, regarding coherence, we should acknowledge the coherence of Castells' vision, which seems altogether more nuanced and cautious than Bell's.

Each of these four points of validity, reliability, comprehensiveness and coherence indicate some limits to Castells' analysis, despite its plausibility.

SUMMARY

Castells argues that:

- far-reaching contemporary social transformation is rooted in the outcome of technological innovation, capitalist restructuring and the search for identity

- the *network society* is a new variant of capitalism

- information is at its core, hence the contemporary era is characterized by an *informational mode of development*

- bureaucracies are transformed into adaptable and flexible *network enterprises*

- in the network society, dominant groups and functions operate in timeless time, while communication technologies eliminate space on a given network

- flows are overlaid on place, and become the prevailing source of power

- new social movements of communal resistance, environmentalism and feminism have replaced the state as a focus of political struggle.

5   CONCLUSION

In different ways, Bell and Castells point to some profound transformations in contemporary society. Both identify the centrality of new technologies to these processes. Bell's work focuses on the changing economy and the rise of the service and information sector, while Castells provides an account which is more concerned with the transformation of time and space.

It is hard not to share with the authors of the work we've explored the feeling that there are some profound social transformations which are underway. As to whether these constitute a new form of society – as Bell and Castells argue – seems more problematic. Few of the phenomena they discuss are entirely new. With most we are talking of an exacerbation, often extreme, of some long-running tendencies. This is exactly what Bell and Castells argue, that the *quantitative* increases in various phenomena together constitute a *qualitative* change, and that the sum of these transformations mean that we live in a fundamentally different form of society. Thus one important way of questioning the utility of the notion of an 'information society' is to ask: at what point does an accumulation of (often dramatic) quantitative changes constitute a qualitative change?

In discussing their work we have raised a number of methodological reservations. In doing so we have seen that our understanding of the information society is achieved through a combination of theory and evidence. Facts don't speak for themselves, but make sense only in the context of some framework, usually a theory. What data are gathered, and how, are decisions made by researchers, largely on the basis of their theoretical concerns and preferences, and their values. It is these issues of methodology which are the subject of Chapter 4. Before that, in Chapter 3, we introduce how social scientists undertake research and the role of values, theory and data in the production of social science knowledge and understanding. We also explore how we can evaluate the work of social scientists.

Social science and the information society

Hugh Mackay and Paul Reynolds

chapter 3

1 MAKING SENSE OF THE INFORMATION SOCIETY

There are many different ways of making sense of social change. We might consult horoscopes, spiritualists, religious leaders, scientists, lawyers, experts in a range of sciences or arts, or others. Each draws on bodies of knowledge and narratives to understand society and to make sense of social life.

This text focuses on a rather different approach – social science. Social scientists seek to understand society by applying a more rigorous approach, though they acknowledge that it is problematic to be scientific about the social world. Social scientists argue that all bodies of knowledge, including the social sciences, are partial and incomplete. They argue, however, that social science provides the basis for *stronger and more persuasive stories* than other forms of understanding the social. David Goldblatt speaks for the social science community in claiming that there exists no significant challenger to social science as a way of describing and analysing societies (Goldblatt, 2000).

In their research, social scientists are involved in the production and critical evaluation of knowledge about society. This chapter explores how social scientists generate social science knowledge and understanding. You will probably have read social science work, but our concern here is to go beyond this, to equip you to understand how social scientists research society, how they make sense of their data, how they evaluate their work, and how their data relate to their theory.

All of us think about, discuss and make sense of social issues and social change. In doing so, like social scientists, we draw on evidence and we develop arguments. Logical argument and the use of evidence are features of common-sense thinking. So in many ways we already use some of the techniques and approach of social science. But common-sense thinking about society is rather different from social science, in three ways. Common-sense thinking tends to be goal-oriented, opinion-driven and concerned with identifying truth. We'll take each of these in turn.

First, common-sense thinking is generally goal-oriented: problems are for solving not reflecting on. A discussion on whether banking on the Internet is safe or not is undertaken for a purpose. It might inform whether you use Internet banking or it might lead you to want banks to address security aspects of Internet banking. The focus of discussion is likely to be on the outcome: safer Internet banking or confirmation that it is not safe enough.

Second, common-sense thinking is opinion-driven: people express their values in addressing social issues. Some people believe a national identity card system backed by computer technology would help to maintain law and order and to identify criminals. Others believe that, whatever the benefits, civil liberties issues make such a system an unacceptable constraint on the freedom of the individual. Both views are based on broader perspectives on freedom and law and order that, in turn, are underpinned by one's values, such as respect for, or criticism of, how the law operates. Values inform judgements in social sciences – as we shall see – but in ways which are rather different from how they do so in common-sense thinking.

Finally, in common-sense thinking there is an assumption that there is a truth – an answer – that can be arrived at, probably with some expert input, by debating opinions. Behind this assumption is the notion that there are principles, laws, ideas or perspectives that are intrinsically right or true. Discussion seeks these truths, which are developed in debate. A truth for many in the Western world is that technology has enhanced our health and lifestyle. Many of us are less receptive of alternative health therapies which assert that our lifestyles, including our increasing reliance on electronic devices such as microwaves, computers and even televisions, are causing illness. Many accept such notions only to the extent that the truth of technological progress is not challenged fundamentally.

Consider common-sense thinking about an aspect of society, for instance, the legislation of cannabis, no-smoking workplaces or traffic calming. Identify in your chosen issue the three features of common-sense thinking: that it is goal-oriented (to achieve a solution), opinion-driven, and includes an assumption of truth.

Broadly, we can identify three ways in which common-sense thinking differs from social science. First, in common-sense thinking, as we've stated, the focus is on a problem and a solution. In contrast, social scientists examine social issues in a *process of inquiry*: the social scientist formulates, conceptualizes and defines research questions, explores and evaluates the claims of other social scientists about those questions or topics, collects and analyses relevant data, and arrives at some conclusion. The investigation is likely to spark new questions which will inform further inquiry.

Second, because common-sense thinking is opinion-driven, it is concerned to persuade and propagate. Discussion involves presenting opinion and information, with relatively little concern for how this is produced. By contrast, social scientists see themselves as *producers of knowledge*, with an interest in the theoretical positions from which different arguments and assertions arise, in the sources of data available, in how data are handled, and in evaluating competing concepts, arguments and analyses. Whilst social scientists ask questions about social issues to produce useful knowledge, they are interested in how that knowledge is produced as well as its contribution to an argument.

Finally, in common-sense thinking, there is often an assumption that it is possible to find immutable truths about a problem. Such truths legitimate opinion and provide the security of being 'right' for those who claim to speak the truth. Truth emanates from religion, revelation, the deduction of scientific law, or some other knowledge that claims the status of truth. Social scientists today are sceptical of any notion of pre-existing 'truths' waiting to be revealed. They see all knowledge as partial because it is *socially constructed* – it emerges from human inquiry, so (being social) cannot be neutral or objective. Moreover, as sociologists of science point out, knowledge production is shaped by social processes, including the market economy, political objectives, social and cultural priorities, and the practices of scientists. Thus knowledge is best understood as *socially constructed*, rather than simply *scientifically deduced*.

Social scientists are acutely aware that the socially constructed nature of knowledge makes it difficult to examine society scientifically. Social scientists belong to the society they examine, which constrains any scientific objectivity they might be inclined to claim. They are aware that values shape the explanations that they produce. Social scientists' thinking is likely to be informed by a preference for some theoretical positions over others. Also, they are aware that the evidence they collect or use may well be selective, partial and incomplete. In social science one can never explore all sources of data, and researchers will interpret data differently from colleagues with different values, perceptions or theoretical affiliations. More than this, many social scientists today would reject the notion of an objective reality out there which can be recorded, pointing to the links between language, representation and 'reality'. Importantly, social scientists incorporate critical reflections on knowledge in their thinking. In the absence of a scientific truth against which to measure argument, the quality of the knowledge which social scientists produce can only be determined by how they produce it and the integrity of their methods. So social science explanations are formed from a complex interplay of interpretation, theory and data. This is represented in Figure 3.1.

Figure 3.1 represents the fact that our explanations of social phenomenon are shaped by values and understanding, by other social scientists' ideas and theories, as well as by data we have collected. These features of social science allow us to build a model of social science thinking which contrasts it with common-sense thinking. This is represented in Figure 3.2.

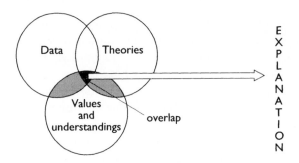

FIGURE 3.1 The building blocks of social science explanation

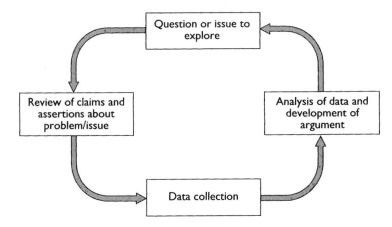

FIGURE 3.2 The social science model of thinking

Figure 3.2 represents the research process. It shows some of the links between theory and data, and between researcher and society, with research generating further issues or areas of inquiry. As David Goldblatt observes: 'The social sciences, both in analysing the world and providing a means for intervention in the world, change and transform their object of study in unintended and unacknowledged ways' (Goldblatt, 2000, p.158).

Social scientists, like others, have their sympathies, preferences and commitments. At the same time, in their work as social scientists, they seek some level of detachment from society to look at how it works. The sociologist Zygmunt Bauman argues that social science requires the researcher to 'defamiliarize' themself, to look with a more open mind at social phenomena to which we are sometimes very close (Bauman, 1990). This defamiliarization may be more or less extreme, but the notion of defamiliarization reminds the social scientist to approach their subject with an awareness of the 'baggage' of their perceptions, experience and values.

Social scientists engage in the rigorous study of society through transparent approaches to how they make their explanations, how they use data and theory, their awareness of the influence of their values, and their reflexivity. They recognize the limits to the knowledge they produce. Social science knowledge and understanding is only as good as its methods.

SUMMARY

Social scientists:

- are interested in *how* we produce knowledge about society as well as what knowledge we produce

- produce knowledge in a *process of inquiry* which involves identifying and defining a question or issue, evaluating how it has been and might be explored, and collecting and analysing relevant data

- generate explanations which draw on theoretical frameworks and empirical data (gathered by others or by the researcher) in relation to a research topic or question

- have values which, in various ways, influence their perceptions, understandings and explanations

- know that any claims that their findings are scientific are limited and depend on the rigour and clarity of their research

- are aware that knowledge is socially constructed.

2   WHAT SOCIAL SCIENCE RESEARCH INVOLVES

We have explained that the quality and persuasiveness of social science thinking depends on the integrity and methods of the research that social scientists undertake. So what does social science research involve? Mirroring the model of social science thinking, social scientists can be seen as engaging in a circuit of research, as shown in Figure 3.3.

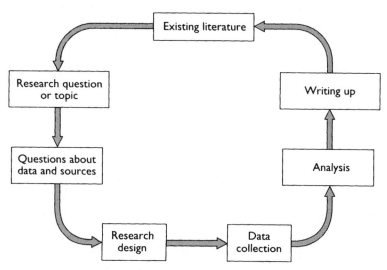

FIGURE 3.3   The research process circuit

The research circuit begins with an idea of something to explore, a hypothesis or a research question. In formulating this the researcher analyses and evaluates the explanations of other social scientists on this or related problems or issues, considering how they collected and evaluated their data. Any research question or topic is contextualized by existing explanations. Then the researcher has to make decisions about their own method of gathering data, to design a research strategy and determine what data to collect and from what sources. After collecting the data, the process moves on to analysing or interpreting the data, and, finally, to writing up the research, addressing the research question or topic. It is worth remembering that at every stage the process is shaped by the theoretical framework within which the researcher is working. While it may seem obvious that our theoretical predilections inform our analysis, it may be less obvious that they shape our selection of a research method.

Decisions about the methods employed, whilst informed by a theoretical position, involve social scientists identifying who or what they want to research, where and when, and the sorts of data they are to gather. Data take different forms, can be derived from a range of sources, and are gathered and analysed in a variety of ways.

Invariably, some combination of one's theoretical perspective and the research question or topic shapes how these decisions are made. To understand patterns of use of mobile telephones, for example, interviews are time consuming. A questionnaire, however, would be a useful instrument for collecting standardized data from a large number of respondents, and fairly quickly. To explore the impact of the mobile telephone industry on the communications industry, one might consult statistical sources on market shares, profits and volume of business, and one might interview key players in the communications industry. To understand how mobiles are perceived as having changed communication behaviour, the best method might be semi-structured interviewing allowing discussion with users about how and why they use mobiles as they do. In each case, decisions about sources of data involve judging what data are required.

Data take several forms. They can be primary or secondary:

- Primary data are gathered by the researcher.

- Secondary data have already been gathered by other researchers.

Data can be quantitative or qualitative:

- Quantitative data are numerical in form, and are measures of volumes, numbers or frequencies. For example, the number of people in an industry, the volume of goods or money produced, or the frequency of Internet start-up failures. Quantitative data are amenable to statistical analysis.

- Qualitative data are concerned with perceptions, feelings or understandings. For example, how social actors make sense of particular settings and interactions. Qualitative research is sympathetic to the concepts and categories used by those being researched rather than (as is usual with a questionnaire) imposing the researcher's categories on the subjects of research.

ACTIVITY 3.1

Look back to the possible ways of researching mobile phones to which we've just referred. Note the different sorts of data (qualitative or quantitative) that would be collected by each of the approaches outlined.

C O M M E N T _____

If you are measuring the volume of mobile phone use you are collecting quantitative data. If you are asking people to explain how they use mobile phones and what they think of how mobiles change the way we communicate, you are collecting qualitative data. The form of data you use depends on the types of question or subject that you want to explore.

We can define data as information. When data are organized, in the context of a research question, they are used as evidence to support or counter an argument. Data are sometimes referred to as facts, but social scientists are wary of such a notion because it implies that the facts speak for themselves.

Social researchers collect quantitative data, qualitative data, or a combination of the two. Statistical sources provide quantitative data. Ethnographic research and semi-structured interviews generally produce qualitative data. Surveys or questionnaires generate quantitative data in 'tick box' or closed questions and qualitative data in the open questions that invite written comments.

Data are the evidence which both supports an argument and contradicts it, but the relationship between theory and data is complex. A researcher might let theory determine what data are collected; or the researcher might try to negotiate the tension between theory and data to both strengthen the theory and to represent the data meaningfully.

To assess the quality of social science research, four criteria of evaluation can be applied: validity, reliability, comprehensiveness and coherence. Generally, the first two of these relate to data, and the second two to theory, or argument. As we shall see, each is more or less applicable depending on the theoretical perspective of the research in question.

- *Validity* is based on the degree to which data measure that which it is claimed they do. For example, to test the hypothesis that mobile telephones, e-mail and other new communication technologies mean that we keep in closer touch with family and friends, we need to establish a direct relationship between use of the new technology and greater or closer contact with family and friends. It is not enough to claim a change in communication technology and to demonstrate an increased volume of use, and then to assume that this means that we keep in touch with family and friends more because, for instance, we might be contacting not family and friends but people we hardly know. Whatever the trend of usage, the researcher would seek to prove or disprove the hypothesis by examining data on who is being communicated with and for what purposes. Validity is about whether we are measuring what we claim to be measuring. Clarity of concepts are an important aspect of validity.

- *Reliability* is about the extent to which repeated measurements using the same research instrument in the same conditions produce the same results. Reliability is tested by repetition. If we claim that mobile telephone users keep in touch with their partners more often than non-users when they are away from home, then reliability would be supported by generating the same finding using a similar but different sample of respondents and on several occasions. Reliable claims are those that can be demonstrated repeatedly. Having said that, social science research is highly difficult to replicate exactly, because contexts, settings and actors are dynamic and ever-changing.

- *Comprehensiveness* is based on the extent to which a piece of research is applicable to all the different cases and contexts to which it is claimed to apply. If a researcher who is exploring mobile phone use claims that mobile phone users have greater contact with their partners when away from home than non-users, they would have to establish that this is the case for all types of users. Is it the same for men and women? Is it the same for younger and older people? Is it the same for people of different ethnicity, sexuality, disabilities, occupations, cultures, or in different countries? The more general a social science claim, the more comprehensive it has to be.

- Finally, *coherence* is based on the extent to which a piece of research is logical and consistent in its line of argument and use of concepts and theory. Tests of coherence explore the logic of the argument. For example, you might be guided in your thinking about new technological communication by a view that the development of new technologies has dramatically transformed social relations. This view might be rooted in the understanding that technologies are shaping social relations and processes (an issue we explored in Chapter 2). If you also assert that particular social interests profit from using or suppressing this technology and have greater power over these technologies than do other social interests, there is something of a logical incoherence in the argument. Is technology determining social processes, or are social interests determining how technology is deployed? The argument might be more coherent if causality is attributed to either technology or social processes or, better, if a more complex model of reciprocal causality is provided. Goldblatt provides a useful way of looking at coherence when he identifies three key tests of accounts of society: the clarity of key claims and concepts, the logic of the chain of reasoning, and the plausibility and accuracy of the hidden assumptions behind the claims and reasoning (Goldblatt, 2000).

Validity, reliability, comprehensive and coherence are the four main criteria with which we can assess or evaluate research. In different social science traditions and studies these carry different meanings and weight, within the broad parameters we have outlined. Together they enable us to judge the plausibility of social science research. We return to them in Chapter 4.

SUMMARY

- Social research addresses a subject, question or hypothesis and uses research techniques to gather data.
- There are two significant decisions to be made in designing social research: sources of data and methods of gathering data.
- There are two broad types of data – quantitative and qualitative – and a range of social science methods to collect each of these.
- There are four criteria that social scientists use to evaluate research: validity and reliability of data, and comprehensiveness and coherence of argument.

3   SOCIAL SCIENCE, RESEARCH AND REFLEXIVITY

We shall conclude this chapter with two issues about the relationship of the social researcher with society. First, social science is linked with action, it is *praxeological*. Researching is itself a form of social action but, more than this, the knowledge and awareness generated by research commonly feeds in to broader discussion and processes of action and change. Social science is not an abstract science but is firmly embedded in society. Commonly, social science motivates action, and moves the researcher into a more active state of mind about the society in which they live.

Second, much social science is *reflexive*. Reflexivity is an approach in social science that departs from positivist approaches and recognizes that the researcher is a part of their research. At one level this means that those who undertake research need to be aware of social processes beneath the surface representations of how society works. More than just more complex understanding, reflexivity can involve standing back and having an awareness of oneself as an observer and as a part of the social processes under investigation. Reflection gives insight into the relation between the researcher, the research subject, and research findings.

The social policy researcher Tim May identifies two forms of reflexivity that complement one another in avoiding a linear model of social science thinking

(May and Williams, 1998). *Endogenous* reflexivity involves recognizing that in any social context there is reflection by social actors upon the social milieu that people inhabit, and this reflection feeds into their actions and social change. This reflexivity reminds us that we cannot easily map causality and reason on to social change and development because the production of knowledge itself has a causal element. *Referential* reflexivity focuses on the interplay between researcher and researched, where knowledge is produced from the act of research and the joining together of different forms of knowledge and knowledge production – research and lived experience, or the 'defamiliarized' (to return to Bauman's concept) and the immediate familiar of social life. This reflexivity cautions the researcher to consider their research as intervention, their place in the research as a variable in the research process, and the production of social knowledge as intertwined with knowledge production and social change. As the sociologist Alvin Gouldner observes:

> A reflexive sociology, then, is not characterized by *what* it studies. It is distinguished neither by the persons and the problems studied nor even by the techniques and instruments used in studying them. It is characterized, rather, by the *relationship* it establishes between being a sociologist and being a person, between the role and the man performing it. A Reflexive Sociology embodies a critique of the conventional conception of segregated scholarly roles and has a vision of an alternative. It aims at transforming the sociologist's relation to his work.
>
> (Gouldner, 1971, p.495)

Gouldner was writing in the 1960s about what he saw as a crisis in sociology. He saw social science becoming absorbed by the corporate agendas of business, government and the academy, and losing sight of the need to understand and be critical of society, in order to improve it. The notion of reflexivity has been elaborated and given more attention by social scientists since then. Reflexivity does not necessarily belong to any of the four perspectives we are outlining, but has been a feature of the shift from positivism.

In this chapter we have sketched the essence of how social scientists undertake research. These methods, principles and issues are generic – they apply across the breadth of social sciences. At the same time, we have put forward the approach that knowledge is socially constructed. This introduction to social science research forms the basis for considering the relationship of theory to data, the focus of Chapter 4.

Researching the information society: methods and methodologies

Hugh Mackay and Paul Reynolds

1 RESEARCH AND ITS METHODOLOGICAL UNDERPINNINGS

In Chapters 1 and 2 we outlined the parameters of debates about the information society and used, in a preliminary way, social science criteria to evaluate claims that we live in an information society. In Chapter 3 we introduced the social science approach to studying, understanding and explaining society and social change. This chapter moves our discussion forward by examining the philosophical underpinnings of social research methods, outlining how the main types of research methods work and how social scientists use research methods to produce social knowledge and understanding. It will elaborate what social scientists do in building explanations and arguments through using research methods. These methods can be understood as the means of gathering data about society, the tools with which social scientists do their work.

To understand how social scientists choose which tools to use, we also need to understand what social scientists think they can know about society. So in this chapter we discuss research methodologies, by which we mean the principles which lie behind research design. A methodology is an approach or perspective which encompasses notions of what we can know about society. Methodology relates to how and what we can find out about society by using research methods, and how far data generated by social research can tell us anything meaningful about society. We shall explore four methodologies of social research: positivist, interpretivist, critical and cultural. As we explore these four approaches, we shall introduce a range of methods, or tools, which are available to social researchers, and shall discuss their strengths and weaknesses. We do this by referring to a policy document on the information society, which in many ways epitomizes prevailing information society discourse – the Wales Information Society (WIS) report, a policy report produced in 1997 by the Wales Information Society Project which is funded by the Welsh Development Agency and the EU.

2 METHODS AND METHODOLOGIES

We began this chapter with a distinction between methods and methodology. A research method is a way of gathering data, such as a survey (for example, the government census or consumer surveys on the goods or services that we buy). For a researcher, methods are the tools of their trade. A research methodology underpins the researcher's choice and use of particular methods on a research project. It encompasses the researcher's understanding of the nature of knowledge that social research can produce. Methodology informs the design of a research project and, more broadly, defines the scope and limits of the production of knowledge by given methods.

The view of social science which we developed in Chapter 3 has tended to regard the study of society as dependent on the rigorous and critical application of research methods. There are no immutable laws of society, no 'truths' to uncover, because knowledge about society is socially constructed – produced by researchers who are social beings. Their values shape their analysis in a diversity of ways, so social science knowledge is contingent upon the perspectives and understandings of the researcher. It follows that we can evaluate social science research only by evaluating the methods used by the researcher.

The WIS report is a policy report, written to influence political and economic decision making. It is a local report on what is a major area of EU and economic development policy. Since we return to this document on several occasions in this chapter, we'll pause to outline it briefly.

The report is bilingual (English and Welsh) and written by John Osmond, the Director of the Institute of Welsh Affairs, it was commissioned by the Wales Information Society Project of the Welsh Development Agency which, in turn, was funded for the purpose by the EU. The purpose of the report is to outline the impact of the information society on Wales and to identify how Wales might benefit from and take some control of the information revolution. It adopts an unquestioning acceptance that an information society has emerged or is emerging. It draws on a range of reports and documents to build its discussion, most of them official publications of the EU or the UK government. The report, like EU policy in this area, is premised on the notion that the information superhighway and ICTs offer considerable benefits in terms of economic growth, new employment opportunities, communications, greater opportunities for a learning society that educates and trains its population, and greater possibilities for the enjoyment of culture and entertainment. It provides a rationale for the Wales Information Society Project and urges businesses, communities, families and individuals to respond positively, to embrace new technologies and to take advantage of the opportunity to build a more economically successful and socially advantaged society. The report is very much a promotion of the Wales Information Society Project, but in promoting the project it makes claims, using data and building arguments about the information society. We shall occasionally refer to how it does this as we introduce each of the four methodologies of social research, starting with the positivist.

3   POSITIVIST PERSPECTIVE

The founders of the social sciences in the nineteenth century did not share the approach to social science thinking and research that we outlined in Chapter 3. They took a positivist perspective on the production of social knowledge. Auguste Comte, whose social physics founded sociology, regarded social science as analogous to natural science. According to this perspective, the social science endeavour is to uncover the immutable laws of society by deducing social facts. Emile Durkheim, another of the founders of sociology, in his *Rules of Sociological Method* (1895), claimed 'our method is objective. It is dominated entirely by the idea that social facts are things and must be treated as such' (Durkheim, 1966, p.143).

Positivist researchers observe social interaction and record and analyse quantitative data in the form of statistics. They argue that social knowledge is only scientific – only valid and reliable – if it is produced by a scientific method, by which they mean experiment or verifiable observation. An experiment is a test of a hypothesis undertaken in controlled conditions in which the researcher seeks to explore the reaction or response to particular stimuli, and to draw conclusions. A verifiable observation is a record of incidence, an event, or an occurrence which can be represented in a quantified form.

According to some positivists, the motives, intentions, values and frameworks of understanding of the researcher are irrelevant, being neither a part of the scientific process, nor verifiable scientifically. They are social fictions, whereas social research is concerned with social facts – represented by quantitative data and collected by quantitative methods such as surveys and statistical analyses. Positivists assume that social cause and effect can be identified by quantitative data and that the researcher can both understand society and make predictions about social change by analysing quantitative data. The key positivist method is statistical analysis, which is commonly combined with the comparative method. As Durkheim claimed:

We have only one way to demonstrate that a given phenomenon is the cause of another ... to compare the cases in which they are simultaneously present or absent, to see if the variations they present in these different combinations of circumstances indicate that one depends on the other.

(Durkheim, 1966, p.125)

A positivist might look at the WIS report and scrutinize its use of statistics to identify the statistically based social transformations it identifies. The report draws on a range of statistical sources to describe the increased use of ICTs, the growth of jobs in IT industries, and the increasing use of the greater volumes of information on the World Wide Web. It uses survey data to identify public and business awareness of the benefits of ICTs and attitudes to, and uses of, computers by members of the various socio-economic classes. A positivist might recognize that the report presents data which support the proposition of an information society but might wish for further data to support its claims. Nonetheless, they might see it as representing some of the strengths of positivist methods, in that it provides a quantitative account of social trends on the basis of verifiable evidence.

Researchers in clinical psychology, demographic studies and other areas approach research in a positivist way. Using statistical data and quantitative methods they tend to see a greater certainty in their findings than in those of researchers who use qualitative methods. However, as social science grew from its roots in natural science, and science itself came under scrutiny for its assumptions of the certainty of social facts, so positivism came under question. In particular, qualitative data gathering methods came to be seen as important for understanding social life and social change.

ACTIVITY 4.1

What are your initial thoughts about the positivist perspective? Note what you see as the limits of positivist, quantitative, research.

COMMENT

Positivist research undoubtedly generates useful data for understanding social change, but three weaknesses can be identified. First, in pursuing what can be measured or quantified, positivists take no cognisance of the more intangible or qualitative aspects of the social, such as motives, intentions and frameworks of understanding. The WIS report, for example, deploys findings of a survey of 1,018 adults from across Wales to identify their awareness of and attitudes to ICTs and the information society. It assumes that attitudes relate to access and ownership of ICTs. But access or ownership do not necessarily reflect attitudes. They might indicate a lack of money to buy a computer. In other words, the 'social fact' of ownership can be interpreted in various ways. But the WIS report, which simply concludes that the information society needs to be promoted in Wales, and particularly among certain groups, does not consider the material basis of exclusion.

Second, positivists assume that social facts fit into self-evident categories. The WIS report draws on European evidence to argue that more jobs will be created than lost in the shift from an industrial to an information economy. It connects job creation with the development of ICT industries without questioning the veracity of these employment categories. For example, flexible, casual and fractional employment are not separated from full-time employment. The category used is simply 'employment'. Though they may use a more segmented set of categories to describe different forms of employment, positivists will always work with categories that make sense to the researcher, and allow the researcher to organize their (quantitative) data. But this might result in misleading interpretations, for example when discussing the experience of information work.

Finally, positivists tend to assume that social facts enable researchers to identify trends and thus to predict social change. This represents a very particular view of the role of the researcher in producing social research. The WIS report draws on official documents and is written to represent and promote the interests of the Welsh Information Society Project. It presumes that developments in ICTs provide opportunities for economic, social and cultural progress. Statistics that show an increasing use of ICTs in business and in the home are represented as positive developments. No qualitative evaluation of such transformations are discussed. The survey commissioned and cited in the report shows that 72 per cent of respondents saw IT as leading to greater efficiency, and 61 per cent saw it creating employment, but there is no definition of efficiency, nor any statement about what respondents understood by this term. Efficiency is assumed to be unproblematic and positive. The survey gathered data on 'efficiency', but did not invite responses on IT in terms of de-skilling or impoverishment. A section of the report discusses the development of call centres as a sign of progress, whereas others might see these in terms of the de-skilling of work or the destruction of local communities (with the closure of local bank branches). In other words, the analysis is shaped by an interpretation of particular social facts and by the use of preconceived categories.

4 INTERPRETIVIST PERSPECTIVE

Such criticisms of positivism developed alongside an alternative methodology for the social sciences – interpretivism. Interpretivism starts from the position that making sense of social change involves understanding the thinking, meanings and intentions of those being researched. Quantifying social action is a limited way of understanding meanings. Positivists might record quantitative measures of e-mail use, to show the growth of the communication medium. They can tell us little, however, about the significance of e-mail communication. They are unlikely to explain whether e-mail is different or the same as other forms of communication, why people communicate more or less by e-mail, or how we should understand e-mail communication, for example, in comparison with telephone calls. To answer such issues and to make sense of e-mail communication, we need to explore the interpretations of e-mail users.

Interpretivists are concerned to understand the social by exploring how people make sense of their life and experience, so they focus on the meanings that people construct in their social interaction. Meanings are produced by individuals whose subjective frameworks of meaning vary. Interpretivists explore the social by examining actors' definitions and interpretations. To do this, they examine the interpersonal construction of meanings in local contexts. The researcher seeks to understand experience by getting close to this, either by first-hand observation or by semi-structured interviews which allow respondents to express their understandings, meanings and motivations. Such observation can take a more active (participant) or more passive (non-participant) form. Clearly, in such a context, although research methods are important, so too are 'everyday' skills. The sociologist Ned Polsky observes that 'Successful field research depends on the investigator's trained abilities to look at people, listen to them, think and feel with them' (Polsky, 1971, p.124).

An interpretivist critique of the WIS report might note that much of the data presented are of trends in ICT use, at work and in the home. Interpretivists would be more interested in the sense made of ICTs. They would be critical of a survey of 1,018 respondents as a means of exploring attitudes, and would see respondents' attitudes as constrained by predetermined questions and categories. Instead they would use interviews to explore respondents' meanings, categories and understandings. Interviews can range from the unstructured (inviting the respondent to lead the session) to the structured (imposing a clear structure and agenda on the interview). Most interpretivist interviews mix these approaches and are *semi-structured*, following a predetermined checklist of topics to be covered, but allowing the interviewee to shape the order, pace and structure of the interview. This contrasts with the highly structured WIS survey. Interpretivists would be critical of the part of the survey in which respondents are invited to describe the information society. This elicited only 110 responses, which are reported as commonly vague and inaccurate. Interpretivists would point out the limits of exploring such issues using such a research instrument. They would be critical of the WIS report's interpretation of social change without evidence of the diversity of interpretations of these changes. So positivists and interpretivists in many senses are opposed, with interpretivists gathering qualitative data on a smaller sample and focusing on questions of meaning.

ACTIVITY 4.2

From this brief summary, what are some limitations of interpretivism? Return to Chapter 3, Section 2, and the evaluation criteria of validity and reliability. Note ways in which interpretivist research does and does not meet these criteria.

C O M M E N T

Interpretivists focus on identifying participants' understandings and interpretations. But, first, can researching such subjective matters generate any reliable or comprehensive research findings? Interpretivists make no claims of generalization from the small number of settings which they have investigated in depth. So there is a richness of depth, but how useful are findings which are valid only in the setting where the research was undertaken?

Second, interpretivism focuses on exploring everyday frameworks of meaning. The danger here is that the idiosyncrasies of the individuals or settings under study become the focus of research. We see the world in the terms and through the eyes of the very small and perhaps atypical sample. Whilst findings which may be interesting are generated, it raises questions about how we understand and evaluate these views. Where is the 'de-familiarization' or detachment to which some social science aspires? From such a position, the danger with interpretivism is that the researcher gets too near to the subject they are exploring and loses critical distance. It can be argued that a research method should facilitate social understanding beyond both an ostensibly objective perspective that privileges the researcher's view and a subjective introspection where all views researched are equally valid.

Finally, interpretivists tend to be sceptical regarding the very notion of social science. One of the strengths of interpretivism is to recognize that the researcher as well as those being researched will have frameworks of meaning that shape the research. This is not the same, however, as saying that social research is analogous to everyday experience, observation or discussion. Interpretivists generally attempt to establish criteria to test validity and reliability, for example in examining the framework of meaning of a member of a specific group. Interviews and observation follow a form to avoid their degeneration into impressionistic reportage. Interpretivism constructs explanations from the interpretations of individuals or groups, but it does not abandon the idea that we can apply methods rigorously or employ criteria of evaluation to strengthen our understanding of the social.

5 TRIANGULATION AND MULTIPLE METHODS OF DATA COLLECTION

We can summarize important aspects of our discussion so far by comparing and contrasting qualitative and quantitative data. This is done in Table 4.1.

TABLE 4.1 Distinguishing quantitative and qualitative methods

	Qualitative	Quantitative
Methodology	Interpretive	Positivist
Forms of data	'Soft' – meanings and interpretations	'Hard' – statistics
Claimed character of data	Value-laden	Value-free
Flexibility (whether respondent can influence the use of the research method)	Flexible (such as semi-structured interviews)	Inflexible (such as surveys)
Focus of analysis	Subjective perceptions	Objective phenomena
Sample	Case studies	Larger populations
Research context	Grounded in social context and interested in actors' categories	Based on researcher's predetermined categories
Methods	• Interview • Participant or non-participant observation • Textual analysis • Semi-structured interviews • Focus group • Ethnography	• Questionnaire survey • Experiment • Structured and recorded observation • Measurements of volumes and frequencies

Although we have tried to delineate methodologies and to associate them with particular methods, in practice researchers commonly deploy a variety of methods. A survey, for example, usually has both closed questions that yield responses that can be tabulated or represented statistically, and open questions, where respondents can provide more qualitative data. Exploratory interviews might inform the design of a survey, or observation might prepare the researcher for an interview.

The use of multiple methods or sources in social research is often referred to as triangulation. Triangulation involves using more than one method to produce different forms of data, or the same method to gather data from different sources. The data can be compared, and similar findings from different methods or sources may support the validity and comprehensiveness of an argument. The purpose of triangulation is to support the reliability and validity of data, and the coherence and comprehensiveness of arguments.

How might triangulation have improved the research on attitudes to ICTs in the WIS report?

The researchers might have undertaken a survey to confirm whether their categories had any relevance for respondents. A pilot study is a small-scale study to test a research instrument, be it an interview schedule, questionnaire survey, or observation techniques. It allows fine-tuning before a full study is undertaken. In this case, the researcher might have triangulated by undertaking participant observation in a workplace or Internet café. If these methods yielded data to support the survey finding that ICTs are seen as tools that make work more efficient and leisure more enjoyable, then such an argument would have greater validity and reliability.

Selecting a method and the balance between methods is often influenced by the resources and time available to the researcher, but also by their methodological predispositions, or the research paradigm within which they are working.

6 CRITICAL PERSPECTIVE

A third perspective has emerged that provides a cautionary caveat to both positivism and interpretivism – the critical perspective. The best known examples of this perspective are the critical theory of the Frankfurt School and feminist perspectives. The Frankfurt School is a school of Marxist thought that argues that researchers should foreground the social context within which they undertake their research, namely the power relations and structural inequalities of capitalism. Feminist perspectives focus on gender as the defining basis of inequality and oppression in society. Both Marxist and feminist researchers focus on the research context – the power relations and structural inequalities in society – and on the potential uses or mis-uses of their research. They see research as inextricably linked to struggle against oppression – an example of the praxis we discussed in Chapter 3. As Marx and Engels observe at the end of *The German Ideology*, 'The philosophers have only interpreted the world, in various ways: the point is to change it' (Marx and Engels, 1932/1998, p.170). The cultural geographer David Harvey expands this notion: 'At the heart of critical social research is the idea that knowledge is structured by existing sets of social relations. The aim of critical methodology is to provide knowledge which engages the prevailing social structures. These social structures are seen by critical social researchers ... as oppressive structures' (Harvey, 1990, p.2).

Critical researchers use the same methods as positivists, interpretivists, or others, but deploy these to contribute to the emancipation of the oppressed or to understand some form of exploitation. Their theory and values guide the shaping of research questions and other stages of the research process.

Critical researchers argue that positivist and interpretivist researchers have three weaknesses. First, in undertaking their research they ignore its social context – interpretivist researchers because they focus on a local setting and so do not explore broader structures, such as the exploitation of capitalism (for Marxists) or patriarchal oppression (for feminists). For example, critical work on the information society might explore the prevailing assumptions that the information society represents progress by unpacking what sort of progress it offers and for whom.

Second, critical researchers criticize much positivist and interpretivist research for engaging in social research without a coherent theory of structured power; they treat all social subjects as of equal worth, disregarding social divisions and inequalities. Even positivist or interpretivist research that identifies class or gender as a relevant variable does not necessarily grasp the structured nature of class or gendered inequalities. This is illustrated by the WIS report's failure to explore the class basis of access to, and uses of, ICTs and the Internet. It shows little sensitivity to the notion that the exclusion of members of the working class might not be because they have failed to grasp some information message but because they lack access to IT resources and the associated skills.

Finally, critical researchers might raise questions about the impact of prevailing power structures on the research process and research findings. They might point to the interests of those who generate the data and reports on which the WIS report draws. Most of these reports are prepared by European technocrats or academics who achieve status through producing research outputs, so they have some investment in the changes they describe. Such a context shapes the knowledge which is generated, but also the frameworks of understanding which are used by researchers.

A common feminist critique of much social research is that it fails to acknowledge the significance of gendered relations. In a patriarchal society men have power in social institutions, and male values, stereotypes of gender relations and male-dominated language and culture are significant in the production of social knowledge, thus excluding women and subordinating them to male agendas. The feminist sociologists Liz Stanley and Sue Wise argue that positivists and interpretivists make assumptions about social subjects based on stereotypical definitions of masculinity and femininity (Stanley and Wise, 1993). Both positivists and interpretivists fail to see gender as a significant variable throughout the research process, and assume that knowledge is gender-neutral.

It is noticeable that the WIS report makes no significant reference to gender, race, disability or other social divisions in discussing the benefits of the information society. Like most such reports it paints a picture of society from a male perspective and rooted in male values. There is no critical analysis of how patriarchy shapes social research, reflects male dominance and reinforces women's exclusion. It does not address the gendered nature of work, and the report's graphics constitute stereotypical representations of gender roles.

Critical perspectives provide significant insights into how social knowledge is produced, linking research to its structural context. At the same time, they create two difficulties. The first is that if theory leads research, there is a danger that research findings simply confirm the theory. If you start a research project with an assumption that class is the primary structure in society, it is highly likely that your research findings will reflect that foundation. Research can become little more than an illustration of a theoretical argument, substantiating the researcher's theoretical predisposition. Thus, regarding the subject of the WIS report, questions of class and patriarchy might be seen as more important or central than any information revolution, or than transformations not obviously congruent with a class- or gender-based analysis.

The relationship between theory and method relates to a broader question: how do we choose the correct methodology for exploring a particular social phenomenon? The sociologist Martin Bulmer identifies four responses to this question (Bulmer, 1984).

1   The researcher can select a methodology appropriate to the problem identified. For example, to understand economic development one might focus on statistical data on profitability, market share and volumes of production and the positivist perspective associated with such quantitative data.

2   It can be selected on the basis of the theoretical position of the researcher. For example, feminist researchers might adopt interpretivist methods and a critical perspective.

3   It can be selected on the basis of the methods expertise of the researcher. For example, a researcher specializing in observation and interviews is likely to develop a theoretical position congruent with interpretivism.

4   It might be selected on the basis of the researcher's methodological position. For example, a positivist researcher will generally look to methods that yield quantitative data.

These four possibilities might operate in conjunction with one another. The point is that theory and the choice of methods in social research are closely linked. Theory is not simply the product of social research, but should inform social research transparently and be subject to modification in the light of research findings.

The second problem raised by critical perspectives relates to the notion that research is emancipatory or revolutionary. There is a tension between addressing a radical agenda by undertaking research which will inform progressive social change and political struggle, and at the same time engaging in de-familiarization to avoid bias. This is rather different from the notion that research begins with an issue, informed by a theoretical position, and explores and examines that issue. Rather, research is to serve a more narrowly conceived aim, to promote a particular political priority. Clearly this raises questions about the relationship of evidence to argument, and the critical evaluation of research findings.

Having said that, critical perspectives offer two important strengths. First, they stress the importance of the social and historical context of research – going beyond positivist and interpretivist approaches. Second, they reinforce the notion that the researcher's role is critical and has an impact on research findings, and therefore involves some responsibility.

7 CULTURAL PERSPECTIVE

Recent developments in social and cultural theory constitute a fourth perspective, one critical of positivist and interpretive approaches for their claims to yield valid and reliable data, and of critical perspectives for fitting data into a priori, **reductionist** arguments.

Reductionist
By reductionist is meant the reduction of complex social processes to some key concepts, such as class or gender.

In recent years there has been what is sometimes referred to as a 'cultural turn' or 'discursive turn' in the social sciences. The social sciences have been strongly influenced by cultural studies, a loosely defined subject area which links post-structuralist literary traditions with the social sciences. There has been a dramatic growth of scholarly interest in culture, which is defined in several different ways. For some, culture is that which is opposed to the biological: drawing on anthropology, human behaviour is seen as shaped by culture, not genes or biology. Others see culture as opposed to nature, and synonymous with civilization – and to be contrasted with barbarism, state and institutional interaction, or mass society. Others are interested in culture as something which is opposed to structure: culture provides the framework which binds society together. Others see culture as something opposed to the material: rather like ideology, it is the beliefs and practices of a society. Finally, and again drawing on anthropology, culture is seen as about a way of life – hence researchers focus on everyday life and popular culture. None of these concerns is especially novel but, together and combined with an approach to research, they constitute something of a new perspective in social sciences, as we shall explain.

Research on culture deploys an eclectic range of methods. Generally, however, these focus on language, representation and discourse. Meanings are constituted in and through language and other systems of representation. Discourses – at one level simply passages of connected writing or speech – are seen by the French philosopher and historian Michel Foucault as systems of representation which regulate the meanings which can and cannot be produced. In other words, Foucault's notion of discourse provides something of a new model of power which operates on and through people by means of discourse; it is not something rooted in institutions, a material structure, or 'out there'. Rather, through linked statements which constitute a way of representing and regulating meaning, language is linked with practice, truth is constructed, and power is exercised. What passes as truth depends on its specific historical context; for example, what passes as 'madness' has varied enormously across time – 'madness' has never existed outside the discourse that has constructed it. Thus knowledge is linked with power, and representations have to be understood in the context in which meaning is produced.

Research on culture has generally focused on reading texts – by which is meant not simply literature or prose, but any cultural artefact. By 'reading' is meant exploring the meanings communicated, which involves exploring sites and practices of both production and consumption, the encoding and the decoding of texts; and intertextuality, the ways in which meanings are constructed by reference to other texts or genres.

We shall explore the methods and concepts of discourse and textual analysis in some detail in Chapter 5. For now, we should note that recent work on the study of culture problematizes social science notions of truth, reality and knowledge. In many ways, cultural approaches can be seen as a response to understanding the late modern or postmodern condition. They have led to some rethinking of what in the past has passed for rigour, validity, reality and truth, and to the development of interpretive and reflective approaches.

From such a cultural perspective, the WIS report and social science critiques might be understood as attempts to impose particular ideas and knowledges – in this case the orthodoxy of the information society – upon their readers. Knowledge producers – and that includes social scientists – impress their stories upon others and exclude voices that might otherwise be heard.

Undertaking a textual analysis of the WIS report, we can make a number of observations about its rhetoric and narrative – its language and story. The report is part of a genre (official reports) and adopts a form that is congruent with our expectations of these – an interplay of statistics as facts and narrative to explain a state of affairs and to set up an agenda for action. Its form and genre encourage people to accept it. Reading the report we can see that:

- Although the information society is the focus of the report, the term is neither defined nor used with clarity. It is subject to a confusion of interpretations.
- The language of the report shows a technological determinism in seeing the information society – social change – as a consequence of technological development, and in seeing the development of particular technologies as inevitable.
- The language deployed is normative and positive, underlining the desirability of the information society.
- Many of the visual images are of new technology and make positive associations with high-tech modernity.
- The use of technical terms and a glossary which define these, sells the message of the information society by drawing the reader into the language.

- The use of data is highly unsystematic, and links only very loosely with the argument of the report. However, such data are a narrative device to suggest a factual basis for what are really rather loose conjectures.

- The rhetoric mystifies the information society in selling a narrative of progress.

We can speculate on the possible interests of those who propagate such reports which lay claim to document and elaborate social change. It is easy to see the WIS report as a contribution to a discourse that obscures self-interest in the guise of neutral and inevitable social change.

Importantly, however, we might also wish to reflect on the interest we have as researchers in such reports. The reflexive practitioner will wish to consider the possibly disparate cultural influences on their work and their investments in particular topics or ways of working. In this sense, social science research too has been subject to re-evaluation in the light of the cultural turn.

ACTIVITY 4.3

You may be unfamiliar with cultural approaches and textual analysis, so it may be worth re-reading Section 7. As you do so, note the implications of cultural approaches for social science.

COMMENT

Cultural approaches make two key contributions to understanding social science methods. First is the relationship between representational practices (and language) and how we understand and make sense of the world. Second is the notion of discourse, and the links between knowledge and power.

In the process, cultural approaches – by focusing on representation and power/knowledge – raise important issues about the nature of social scientific knowledge. In many ways they problematize earlier understandings of social science and notions of validity and reliability in particular. Cultural approaches set an agenda for some initial interrogation of the research process and social science thinking.

We have introduced debates about how the information society and contemporary social change are conceived (in Chapters 1 and 2) and we have introduced some key issues regarding how social scientists make sense of the social and how they undertake research (in Chapter 3 and in this chapter). The next three chapters explore three core themes of information society debates in some detail, and how social scientists have undertaken research in these areas. The three themes are: culture, representation and identities; new patterns of work and inequality; and time–space reconfiguration. In each chapter, we introduce and critically evaluate significant research on the theme.

Culture, representation and identities

chapter 5

Wendy Maples

1 INTRODUCTION

The first core theme we can identify in information society debates concerns the growth of information and communication technologies (ICTs) and their capacity to circulate ever-greater volumes of text, graphics and moving images. In this chapter, we examine three studies which consider the growth of ICTs and the changing nature of representation in the information society. Each study addresses in different ways the links between culture, representation and identities.

Particularly during the past 25 years, the world has become increasingly media-saturated. Broadcast media have grown like never before. There is now a multitude of channels – local, national and global – which arrive by a plethora of broadcasting systems – terrestrial, cable, satellite and the Internet. While broadcasting has been expanding, ICTs in the home have become increasingly interactive: this and **narrow-casting** may prove an effective challenge to the growth or dominance of conventional broadcast media. Older print media have also been transformed technologically, leading to an explosion of advertising, book and periodical publishing. Accompanying this has been a rise in the use of home computers, DTP (desk-top publishing) programmes and easy-to-learn graphics packages, making small-scale publication more accessible than ever before.

Narrow-casting
As opposed to broadcasting, narrow-casting involves targeting specific demographic or lifestyle groups, using media channels such as cable or satellite, and often on a pay-for-view basis.

At the same time as the growth in ICTs there has been tremendous social change. 'Social change' is often understood in terms of political and economic change, changes in the distribution of power and income, changes in work and production. These have certainly taken place, but fascinating cultural changes have also occurred.

For instance, home is still a place where we might sit in front of the fire, but it is now more likely to be where we sit in front of the television or the computer. So, in some ways, day-to-day routines have changed. In addition to this, the boundaries and types of experiences available to us have shifted. Through the use of different ICTs, we've gained a greater exposure to, for example, fashion and design, both of which have increasingly pervaded society: 'image' has acquired a greater significance than ever before. Our sense of image is derived in multiplicitous ways and is enacted on a daily basis in the ways we choose to dress, wear our hair, participate in different social and cultural events, decorate our homes and gardens, and so on.

This suggests that changes in culture and identity are interrelated. Instead of traditional identities relating to nationality, gender and generation acting as dominant cultural determinants, there are a variety of identities from which we more actively choose (see Castells, 1997). Culture and beliefs are no longer confined to geographical locality but are shared and dispersed across nations and continents. An individual's identity is no longer seen as 'static' or 'fixed for all time'; instead, identities are re-articulated and reconstituted throughout the lifecycle. ICTs are seen as instrumental in this regard, with some theorists suggesting our identities are increasingly intertwined with computers, to such an extent that we are becoming 'cyborgs'. This is the more extreme view, but at a more banal level, ICTs are now firmly ensconced in our everyday lives and, arguably, contribute to our sense of self.

ACTIVITY 5.1

Look back at the list you made of ICTs in your home (Chapter 1, Activity 1.3). Which items are 'new' (acquired in the last five or so years)? Have any of the items (old or new) been used in 'new' ways, or do they have different functions from five years ago? (For example, you may have had a home computer for more than five years, but only recently started to use it for accessing the Internet.)

COMMENT

You might have noticed how quickly new ICTs have made themselves at home in your household. On the other hand, perhaps you think that a good deal of what you have is 'old'. Of course, this is a relative term. When my computer broke down, I took it to be repaired. Repair was, apparently, 'economically non-viable' as replacement parts were now difficult to obtain and expensive. Described as 'prehistoric' by the engineer, my computer was all of five years old.

While the pace of change is felt more keenly by some than others, it is certainly a key feature of contemporary society. Yet, the desire to be modern is nothing new – the discourse of 'progress' has been with us for a long time. But how we understand progress, what it means to be 'modern' or, conversely, 'behind the times' now takes different forms. Moreover, representations of how to keep pace are myriad and ubiquitous. But these representations do not go unchallenged. You might feel that having new technologies in your home is essential – adverts about the latest DVD (digital video disc) technology may 'speak to you'. Or you may feel that these technologies and adverts for them are largely irrelevant to your everyday life. Whichever, this suggests an important interplay between culture, representation and identities that circulates around ICTs. In addition, ICTs facilitate the dissemination of culture – not by fiat, edict or propaganda but through signification, or representational practices. Such practices form an important part of the material through which identities are constructed and expressed.

In this chapter we introduce some key concepts in debates about culture, representation and identities and discuss specific research studies. In so doing we also evaluate their research methods. The next section considers in more detail the relationship between culture, representation and identities and serves as an introduction for the case studies that follow.

2   CULTURE, REPRESENTATION AND IDENTITIES

In the social sciences the word 'culture' is often used in its broadest sense to refer to 'whatever is distinctive about the "way of life" of a people, community, nation or social group' (Hall, 1997a, p.2), including the shared values and meanings of a group or of society.

Identity and culture are closely intertwined. Manuel Castells explains:

> The construction of identities uses building materials from history, from geography, from biology, from productive and reproductive institutions, from collective memory and from personal fantasies, from power apparatuses and religious revelations. But individuals, social groups, and societies process all these materials, and rearrange their meaning, according to social determinations and cultural projects that are rooted in their social structure ...
>
> (Castells, 1997, p.7)

Our culture(s) influences our identity – who we are and who we are not. As Stuart Hall, Emeritus Professor of Sociology at The Open University, notes, 'culture is used to mark out and maintain identity within and differences between groups' (Hall, 1997a, p.4) and gives us an idea of who we are and where we belong.

Explanations of how cultural identities are formed have used the analogy of language. We are not born with an in-built understanding of English, Dutch or Urdu – or of cultural meanings. Cultural meanings are communicated to us and learnt by us through the medium of a common 'language' of sounds, words, visual images, symbols, gestures or rituals that stand for – or 'represent' – particular ideas or feelings. Cultural concepts are encoded in different signs, or symbols, which can be read like any other language and form our common understanding of the society in which we live and by which we identify ourselves as belonging to one culture or another.

This account is rather static, however. It implies that culture is fixed and unchanging, that representations reflect an uncontroversial reality and that an unbroken conveyor belt transmits meanings from one generation or sub-culture to another with little scope for misunderstanding or reinterpretation. An alternative view sees representation as far more ambiguous and shifting – as being concerned as much with the construction of culture as with its reflection – and therefore as a key element in social change. Through the production or consumption of the products of the mass media and uses of ICTs we are all involved in 'practices of representation'. As Stuart Hall explains, according to this view, the media through which meanings are transmitted are not neutral channels down which information flows but themselves play a part in the production of cultural knowledge. We should recognize that: 'Meaning is also produced whenever we express ourselves in, make use of, consume or appropriate cultural "things"; that is, when we incorporate them into the everyday rituals and practices of daily life and in this way give them value or significance' (Hall, 1997a, p.3).

Some commentators see as crucial the influence of ICTs on the circulation and control of representations and cultural meanings. Hall (1997b) demonstrates how representational practices are not random but part of a 'politics of representation' in which meanings are contested by different groups. Historically, representations of the 'other' (loosely meaning non-dominant or less powerful groups) have both reflected and helped to construct ideas of, for example, racial inferiority based on negative stereotypes. But counter-strategies can and have been used to trans-code negative images with new positive meanings. A good example of this is the way the term 'black', which in the predominantly white West has had negative associations, was reappropriated by civil rights activists in the 1960s and early 1970s. The phrase 'black is beautiful' gained currency, challenging previous connotations and acting as a rallying cry of empowerment for politically progressive, anti-racist groups. What this example shows is that representations, and culture more widely, are neither impenetrable nor static. Representations are subject to (re)interpretation and cultures are subject to change.

To explore these ideas and to analyse more precisely the influence of ICTs and representational practices on culture and identity we shall look at some research undertaken by social scientists and evaluate their findings and methods. The next section looks at particular kinds of representations and considers how researchers might investigate 'signifying practices'.

SUMMARY

- Culture, in a broad sense, can be understood as a 'way of life'.
- Identity is shaped by a range of cultural experiences, including our experiences of different representations.
- Representations and the channels through which representations are transmitted are not neutral.
- Representations may serve the interests of particular groups over others.
- The 'politics of representation' (Hall) suggests that there is a struggle over meaning, between groups and across cultures.

3 SIGNIFYING PRACTICES AND TEXTUAL ANALYSIS

At the heart of textual analysis is **semiotics**. Semiotics is the 'science of signs'. Semioticians are interested in how meaning is constructed through language. For Ferdinand Saussure, the European founder of semiotics, at the heart of this understanding was the **sign**. The sign is made up of two parts: the signifier and the signified. Take the example of a hat. The written word 'h-a-t' or spoken sound 'hat' is the **signifier**, the idea of the hat that you now have in your head is the **signified** (the two combined are the 'sign'). If we were standing in the middle of the Arizona desert and a woman on horseback rode by, I might say 'I like her cowboy hat!' This would direct you to what Saussure would call the 'referent'. The **referent** is a real world object to which a given sign refers. It is important to notice that the sign is not naturally occurring: it is arbitrary, agreed upon through cultural convention. After all, in Italian, 'hat' is not 'hat', but 'cappello'.

But there's more: because the sign is not only a sign. The cowboy hat suggests something more than a thing which is worn on the head to keep the sun off. The **denotation** of a cowboy hat is *just* that: a clever object that protects its wearer from the sun's excesses. But the **connotation** is something more.

Consider a more particular cowboy hat, one that is white and worn by an actor in a Western movie. That hat or, rather, its connotations, tell you a lot about the character. The character in the white cowboy hat is the good guy. Conversely, the character with the black hat is up to no good.

But there's more still, because we are now examining the conventions of a particular film **genre**. Without going into detail, the good guy/bad guy distinction is evident not because 'real' good guys wear white hats, but because the conventions of the Hollywood Western dictate that they do so. Producers (directors, scriptwriters, etc.) of such films know that their audiences will be able to 'read' this convention, and so reproduce it. In other words, producers infuse their film with shorthands like 'white hats = good guys' expecting their audiences to understand this.

In this particular instance, the white hat connotation draws on a deeper level of meaning within Western culture. Further associations with 'whiteness' are purity, cleanliness, and moral righteousness. But it is not just good guys who wear white. Thinking about the colour white and the cowboy in the Hollywood Western suggests a set of associations that are different to those inferred from the wearing of white by a woman on her wedding day. White connotes purity in both instances, but purity for a bride is different from purity for a cowboy. The difference, of course, has to do with particular cultural conceptions of gender and sexuality and the context within which white is worn.

Semiotics
Semiotic analysis involves unpacking the meaning of signs.

Sign
Made up of signifier and signified, signs carry meaning and are established by convention – they are arbitrary.

Signifier
The combination of letters, sounds or graphics, etc., that indicate, by convention, a signified. One half of a sign.

Signified
The idea of a thing, conjured up by the signifier. One half of a sign.

Referent
A real world object, idea or action to which a sign refers.

Denotation
Simple description of characteristics of a thing, devoid of significant meaning.

Connotation
Meaningful associations of a thing, as distinct from its denotation.

Genre
Often used to classify types of films, genre describes a 'generic type', which we expect to conform to particular conventions, in terms of, for instance, plot, characters, music, settings, etc.

Signification
The practice of producing representations.

Signification draws upon and re-presents a wider set of cultural assumptions or ideals. Where these are regularly – or ritually – confirmed, we come to find them acceptable, normal or natural. Additionally, however, they are in some ways prescriptive, or ordering. Interestingly, whiteness is also defined by its opposite: whiteness is 'not blackness'. This binary becomes a means by which both whiteness and its 'opposite', blackness, are defined – white/black, and their contingent binary connotations: good/bad, pure/impure, etc. We have moved quickly from simple observations about the use of colour to sets of meanings which are deeply culturally subjective, arbitrary and important. The binaries involved are not neutral; they reflect – and help construct – particular sets of ideas which serve some people often to the detriment of others.

Representations
Sometimes written as *re-presentations*, these are the written, oral, graphic or other ways in which meaning is expressed. As re-presentations, they are not neutral, but are inflected with the ideas and concerns of their producers and their time.

Often meanings are constructed through a range of **representations**, not all of which are so immediately readable as the white cowboy hat. Meanings are circulated through culture in complex ways that reflect historical traditions and the inflection of particular circumstances in specific times and places. Yet, through this, certain ideas or themes come to hold special currency.

According to the cultural theorist Roland Barthes, part of our enculturation involves the adoption of what he calls 'myth' (Barthes, 1972). In Barthes' sense, myth is definitely *not* 'untruth' or 'misguided beliefs', as is often perceived in Western, predominantly Christian, cultures. Instead, myths are stories which act as markers of 'truth'. They are the vehicles by which cultural ideas are carried. Barthes argues that:

> Semiology has taught us that myth has the task of giving an historical intention a natural justification, and making contingency appear eternal ... What the world supplies to myth is an historical reality, defined ... by the way in which men have produced or used it; and what myth gives in return is a natural image of this reality.
>
> (Barthes, 1972, p.142)

Barthes was interested in how popular representations, in newspapers, magazines or advertisements could be subjected to textual analysis, using a deeply interpretive semiotics, as myths of our culture. By 'text' he means not only written words or educational material but also rituals or ceremonies, films, clothing, art, garden designs, architecture, TV programmes, hairstyles or advertisements, in fact anything that can be 'read' as having cultural or symbolic meaning. An image, artefact or ritual can reveal quite a lot about a culture and the identities that are acceptable (good cowboys wearing white) and that might pose a challenge to conventions (brides wearing orange). The cultural shock of a symbolic challenge to convention derives not from the artefact, of course, but from the (arbitrary, but powerful) meanings with which it is imbued.

A somewhat different way of thinking about signifying practices is to consider representation, identities and culture in terms of 'discourse'. The enigmatic philosopher and historian Michel Foucault developed the concept of discourse in part as an attempt to move away from what he saw as the rather flat and ahistorical investigations of semiotics. For Foucault, an investigation of meaning was necessarily an investigation of *struggle*, as meaning, or knowledge, is intimately connected with power.

Foucault used the term '**discourse**' in a novel way, not in the conventional linguistic sense of 'passages of connected writing or speech' (Hall, 1997a, p.44). He was concerned with language and certainly felt, as Hall explains, that: 'Discourse is about the production of knowledge through language. But ... since all social practices entail meaning, and meanings shape and influence what we do – our conduct – all practices have a discursive aspect' (Hall, 1992, p.291).

In other words, discourses, or ways of thinking and being, exist throughout all cultural and social practices. Certain discourses gain greater currency in particular historical periods.

Foucault was particularly interested in the ways in which madness, punishment and sexuality were the subject of different discourses over time. In different historical periods, punishment, for instance, came under the jurisdiction of the church/God, local community sanction, crime professionals, such as the police, and state legislators (Foucault, 1977). At the time, each of these groups appeared to be the natural repositories of criminal sanction. Each, however, defined criminality differently and sought different forms of discipline. Foucault attributes these shifts to changes in discursive regimes. Today, there are any number of discourses that construct meaning and meaningful practice, but there are some which are particularly powerful or prevalent.

Consider the common appreciation of new technology. Technology is associated positively with progress and modernity. On a level which might seem rather banal, the availability of new technologies is seen as a generally good thing: we like having new gadgets, telephones, computers or automated anythings. Importantly, this has led to government policies that generally favour new technologies over old. Discourse describes the way certain ideas or behaviours come to have a power or authority that is accepted in a given historical moment as natural. However, as noted above, Foucault saw knowledge as being about struggle. Certain discourses may be powerful or pervasive, but they are not absolute and for all time. This is because social and cultural changes lead to contestations of prevalent discourses. Foucault argues that the seeds of counter-discourse are contained within the discourse itself. As the Luddites demonstrated, and as alternative technology groups continue to reason, new technologies are not necessarily a good thing – concerns about job losses or the environment may militate against a wholesale appreciation of the joy of (new) technologies. In this case, there are competing discourses (to do with employment rights or the environment) which challenge the (currently dominant) discourses that privilege new technologies.

Discourse
Foucault's concept of a system of representation, including language, which regulates the production of meaning at both everyday and institutional levels.

ACTIVITY 5.2

Using the tools of textual analysis introduced above, examine the advertisement which is reproduced in Figure 5.1.

- What is the signifier?
- What is the signified?
- What is denoted by the images and text?
- What do you think is connoted?
- Does the advertisement 'work' on a mythological level?
- What discursive themes might have helped to construct this advertisement?

COMMENT

The advertisement, taken from a broadsheet newspaper's Saturday supplement, is made up of several elements. Keeping this in mind, we shall make a textual analysis of some of its key features.

The central image is of a woman, walking in front of highly reflective glass doors, on which the street signs of a busy city, Hong Kong, are reflected. The main written text says simply 'Know.', while the anchoring text below lists a series of items about which the reader or the central character, might wish to know. The signifier, at its most basic level, is the paper and print of the advertisement, organized into a series of images. The signified, again, at a very basic level, is the woman and her surrounding environment, including the graphics, texts and blank spaces – the advert. At a basic denotative level, there is a woman walking through the visually busy streets of Hong Kong. But this already makes presumptions. There are clues directing us to think she is in Hong Kong. The expression on her face is happy, serene; whilst all around her is visually overwhelming, suggesting a high level of potential confusion. Of course, the advertisement connotes that her serenity comes from 'knowing' and that her knowledge has been gained through the use of her pocket PC.

At the levels of myth or discourse, the advertisement is rather more interesting. This is a fairly young woman and the implication here is that to know does not require the experience of age. This is a play on the myth of age and wisdom: the truth being that in the contemporary moment youth is the repository of wisdom. Knowledge simply requires the right technology. Moreover, knowledge is foregrounded as important at a global level: wherever we are in the world, we need to be connected to a global information infrastructure. This advertisement is, then, also about the global information age and learning to function in it across perceived cultural boundaries. A significant element of the discourse elevates information and communication technologies: they are the keys to a wider world. This discourse about the relationship between security in the world and new technology is one with which we might be familiar from a range of different cultural and political debates: it certainly crops up in the arms race (national security), and is a regular feature of discussion in the increasingly global higher education system

Know where to get the train to Shanghai.*
Know about 100,000 phone numbers.
Know the sound of your baby's laughter.
Know you can read and respond to e-mail from Hangzhou.*
Know millions of websites.*
Know people, places, things.
Know the new HP Jornada Pocket PC.

Know more. Digital information from hp. www.hp.com
www.hp.co.uk

FIGURE 5.1   Advertisement for the Jornada pocket PC

Discursive formation
When a particular set of concepts or ideas become pervasive throughout a range of social institutions and cultural practices.

(individual or institutional security). In Foucault's terms, the evidence of this discourse across a range of subjects suggests a **discursive formation**. The advertisement carries several secondary ideas as well. What is the head-scratching figure (lower left) 'doing' in the ad? You may have noticed 'baby's laughter' as an apparent anomaly in the list of 'things to know'. Other readings might make more of the fact that the central character is female and might draw further inferences from the fact that the majority of early users of new ICTs are young men. Others might spend more time looking at the typeface in the advertisement, or the improbability of some of the reflections (for instance, that the words in English are the right-way-round, not mirrored).

For the advertisement to 'work' for the advertisers, the connotations you infer must be those intended by the advertisers. Remarkably, this is often the case, but it isn't always. Differences in cultural backgrounds, attitudes and expectations are likely to influence interpretations of a given advertisement: different **subjectivities** or identity positions will produce different readings. That said, some readings are more convincing or plausible than others. This plausibility is crucial in social science research. Not only must researchers attend to their studies with care, they must also convince others of the logic or coherence of their reasoning.

Subjectivities
Similar to the idea of identity positions, Foucault argues that discourses produce subjectivities, or ways of being, which we adopt as 'natural'.

This point about the limitations of textual analysis as a method of research reinforces some of the issues raised in Chapter 3:

- The researcher has a proactive role in reading the text, in what is a subjective interpretation. This raises problems regarding possible claims of validity and reliability.

- Textual analysis involves reading the complex codes of representations, where more than one reading or interpretation might be made, albeit with varying plausibility.

- The analysis is of interpretations of a given text by specific readers, making no claims of generalizability or comprehensiveness of research findings.

One other point is that textual analysis is often used as part of a wider research project, stemming from a particular theoretical perspective. Critical perspectives such as feminism or Marxism might use the methods of interpretivism within the theoretical context of patriarchy or capitalism, which raises important questions about the relationship of theory to data: the data may merely illustrate a preconceived framework. For this reason, it is difficult to assess textual analyses in terms of validity or reliability. Where only one – or a few – texts are analysed, comprehensiveness will be limited. Textual analyses tend to be judged in terms of coherence: how convincing, plausible or carefully reasoned is the analysis in question.

Despite the limitations of textual analysis as a social science method, it is an important method for researchers interested in considering what representations *mean* in a culture. It does, however, raise difficulties. That there is no right or wrong answer means that while one reading may seem more plausible than another, there can be no proof either way. From the position of positivist social science, this level of interpretation is unacceptable. Other social science perspectives, however, prefer qualitative data and analyses for the insights they provide into culture and meaning.

This is crucial because what lies behind textual analysis is a supposition that representations don't merely reflect the cultures in which they are embedded, but are also *constitutive* of culture. In other words, representations are not just presentations of a world which is out there waiting to be discovered. As *re-presentations* they are part of the writing and re-writing of that world. To think of this in a slightly different way, representations as constituents of culture also assist in the constitution of us as subjects of discourse. This is the reason to connect representation and identity. So what advertisers, film producers, fashion gurus and others in the business of interpreting and disseminating culture – cultural intermediaries – are involved in is the creation of different identity positions. Some theorists emphasize the power of the media to produce representations which act in a discursive way – circumscribing how we might think about our culture and ourselves.

At the same time, however, it is important not to overemphasize the power of cultural intermediaries. The tools of interpretation are very similar to the tools of production: both focus on the *construction* of meaning. In recent years, there has been a boom not only of cultural intermediaries acting in the interest of corporate media, but also in the interests of 'oppositional practices' (see, for instance, Adbusters.org). The social sciences, of course, contribute to understanding critical practices which enable both the reading and production of cultural meaning.

SUMMARY

- Signs are arbitrary; they are established by convention.
- Significations are powerful and help to establish and prescribe what is 'normal' or 'natural'.
- Meanings are not fixed – they change over time and may be interpreted differently in different contexts.
- Popular representations, may serve a 'mythical' function (Barthes).
- Representations act 'discursively' (Foucault). That is, they provide a structuring 'language' that enables some ways of thinking/behaving but proscribes others.
- Discourses contain within them the seeds of counter-discourses. This explains, in part, how prevalent discourses come to change over time.
- Textual analysis is one way of unpacking representations, seeing representations as important in terms of their cultural signification and for identities.

4 IDENTITY, REPRESENTATION AND THE WEB

Textual analysis is not the only method of investigating representations and their meanings. Your interpretation of the pocket PC advertisement was, possibly, rather different from ours. Had we compared interpretations across a wide group of people, we would have found a range of different interpretations, including some rejections or refusals of the advertisement's intended message. Although there was likely to be a prevailing interpretation, there would also be alternative interpretations. We would have found that people's demographic characteristics corresponded with the types of interpretations made. For instance, Chinese speakers might have made more of the street signs, interpreting the set as less confusing, non-Chinese speakers would likely find the opposite. Heterosexual men might have focused on the sexual appeal of the model, etc. But how could we find out what different people might make of the advertisement?

One way of finding out what people think or feel is to ask them. In many ways, social scientists follow good social practice in such research: they indicate a genuine interest in people and encourage them to talk about themselves. Of course, it isn't quite that simple, but a good researcher will establish rapport with those they study. This is true whether the researcher has limited face-to-face contact with their subjects (when conducting a survey, for example) or whether the researcher's study involves continuous daily contact over a protracted period of time (in the case of ethnographic fieldwork, for instance).

There is a burgeoning literature on the Internet and identity. Much recent research is on computer-mediated, virtual communities. Other studies have focused on how individuals and groups represent themselves in other Internet forums, such as fan pages, discussion groups or personal homepages. We've chosen to examine two areas of research: personal homepages on the World Wide Web and multi-user domains, or MUDs.

Form
The framework of a cultural artefact, which helps shape its content.

Content
Cultural artefacts can be examined in terms of both form and content. Content concerns the particular elements that fill the 'structure' or 'form' of a given artefact.

Research on homepages might begin with an analysis of the **form** and **content** of the web pages themselves. This will be our starting point. But to develop a clearer understanding of the meanings constructed in personal homepages, it will be necessary to extend our research methods. To do so, we look at the work of Daniel Chandler and Dilwyn Roberts-Young who have studied adolescents' web pages and conducted online interviews with the authors of such sites. First, though, we look at a textual approach to homepages, considering a study of personal homepages conducted by new media researcher, Charles Cheung.

According to Cheung, 'a personal homepage is a website produced by an individual (or couple, or family) which is centred around the personality and identity of its author(s)' (Cheung, 2000, p.44). Initially, concerned to identify the different elements or features of a homepage, Cheung accessed a number (he does not tell us how many) of homepages and discerned categories, or types, of personal information they contained. According to Cheung, they include:

- diary, journal, or autobiography

- 'description' of the author's personality

- views on personal, social, political and cultural issues

- personal photographs

- achievements and awards

- places of living and working

- information on and links to personal interests

- links to websites created by acquaintances, friends and family members

- links to websites created by organizations and schools with which the author is or has been affiliated.

(Cheung, 2000, p.44)

Coming up with a series of categories by which a researcher then seeks to define and quantify the interests or aims of similar texts is part of a method known as 'content analysis'. This form of textual research, though relying for the most part on quantifications of content, nevertheless may require a fair degree of interpretation. Ultimately, the researcher will ask: 'What does this mean?', at which stage the content analysis may be subject to a more qualitative textual analysis.

Having established the types of content one might expect to find in a personal homepage, Cheung points out that, ultimately, personal homepages are constructed with a basic question in mind: 'What am I going to put on my page?' Put another way, this question asks: 'What aspects of my "selves" should I present on my webpage?' (Cheung, 2000, p.45). The homepage acts as a vehicle for self-expression and identity-construction. Seeing web-page construction as a largely voluntary activity, Cheung argues that homepages reflect their authors' understanding of their 'acceptable selves' and may be quite selective in terms of content. Intriguingly, the web-page form allows for multiplicitous selves to be presented, reconstructed or deleted over time. This raises a related point: we must be careful not to assume that the person we 'see' on a personal homepage is the 'real' or 'authentic' person. While Sherry Turkle's research (see below) suggests that most people stick fairly closely to their own 'real world' identities when interacting online, people are also likely to emphasize particular aspects of themselves that they consider to be desirable and to underplay, or omit, aspects that may seem less attractive (Turkle, 1996a). This selection process in itself is extremely interesting and may suggest a great deal about our identities – and our culture.

Cheung contends that the eclectic content of homepages indicates that our identities in the late-modern era are, as Castells avers, increasingly eclectic

(Castells, 1997). Our identities are no longer defined primarily by identity positions regarding age, occupation or class, but instead are 'hybrid' – predicated, certainly, by these aspects at certain times in our lives, but also drawing on identities of interest, relationships, sexuality, gender, race, nationality, leisure activities, political persuasion, locality; and they change over time.

Cheung argues that 'the "selves" we have are composed of multiple identities and the associated contradictory experiences. In late-modern society', he writes, 'it is almost impossible to have a fully unified, completed and coherent "self"; rather, we all tend to have fleeting, multiple and contradictory selves' (Cheung, 2000, p.45).

But on what basis does Cheung make this claim? In his research, Cheung began with a survey of different homepages and conducted an initial content analysis, compiling sets of categories of 'types' of representation made by individuals (or families) on their homepages. He then looked at some homepages in greater detail, conducting a kind of textual analysis.

ACTIVITY 5.3

Log on to the web and find a personal homepage. (You might try a site such as WebRing, at www.webring.org)

- What is most striking about the content of the homepage?
- What are the techniques used to direct you to different aspects of the author's identity?
- What different forms are used in the construction of the page (e.g. written text, photos, graphics, links)?
- To what extent do you feel you have gained a sense of the author's identity?

Alternatively, you could sketch your own homepage.

- What would you include/exclude about yourself?
- What kinds of pictures or graphics would you use to frame or embellish your homepage?

COMMENT

One of the homepages Cheung analysed more closely was Lynda's (www.crosswinds.net/~lyndavandenelzen/HOME.htm) (accessed 6 November 2000). Looking at Lynda's homepage, Cheung observes that the author has presented 'multiple and contradictory selves'. He notes that she makes wide use of the range of 'expressive resources' of the personal homepage: biography, a newsletter, fan activity and links to other websites. Other elements which you might have noticed include, for instance: music, voice-overs and other sound effects; games and other interactive segments; guest books, poetry or quotations; artwork, graphics or photographs. You may also have noticed the use of a range of genre conventions. For instance, many homepages are presented in a way reminiscent of family photo albums, with each photograph 'telling a story'. Or you may have found a homepage that draws heavily on the style of broadsheet or tabloid newspapers or arcade video games.

This suggests two key points. First, that what we have conventionally considered discreet genres are increasingly overlapping, with cross-fertilization between old and new media technologies and forms. The information society is characterized by an explosion of different genres, with rapid cross-pollination between them. A vast range of television hybrids have emerged, including: advertisement-soap operas, soap-dramas, dramatic-comedy, comedy-game shows, and game show-fly-on-the-wall-documentaries. Some obvious (or notorious) examples are: the Gold Blend advertisements, *This Life, The Sins, Have I Got News for You,* and *Big Brother.* Such hybridity is equally evident, if not more so, on the World Wide Web.

Second, homepage authors appear relatively dexterous in executing different media forms and fitting content. While presentation skills are variable, the ability to convey ideas or feelings using a relatively new medium with a certain degree of acumen is apparent.

However, Cheung's research doesn't give a clear sense of what these homepages, or web-based identities, *mean* to their authors: there is only a limited understanding of the representations' cultural or personal significance. This is a limitation of Cheung's research. It is useful in that the descriptions appear to be accurate and the categories he identifies can be deployed effectively in analysing other homepages. His quantitative study demonstrates a degree of validity, reliability and comprehensiveness. But his findings appear speculative. There is a fit between his claims regarding multiple identities and the homepages he cites, but his citations are limited. Lynda's may be a good example of a large number of similar homepages, but we have no way of assessing this without further access to Cheung's data, or by testing his findings by undertaking our own research. In terms of reliability, there is some chance of replicating his work, as homepages may remain online for extended periods, but, as he notes, they are subject to change. Most importantly, for this type of research, Cheung's textual analysis must demonstrate plausibility. In the case of Lynda's homepage, Cheung's theories appear to describe well the elements of its construction: they are plausible. However, if Cheung is concerned primarily with the meanings of the homepage for its producer, we might well ask why he chose to examine representations, rather than speak with producers themselves. Of course, not every study can do everything and Cheung will have made choices about the feasibility of his study which led him to choose textual analysis rather than other, perhaps more time-consuming, methods, but this reflects on the *validity* of the more qualitative aspects of his study.

Daniel Chandler is another theorist of new media (whose work you can consult at: http://www.aber.ac.uk/media). Like Cheung, Chandler argues that constructing a homepage is not simply building a base for communication, but is a construction of the self. Chandler sees the appropriation and creative deployment of web technology as empowering, offering a platform for those otherwise silenced or invisible. But, more than simply a projection of the author into the public sphere of web communication, it allows the author to appropriate signs and symbols from the public domain, and to use these in the service of identity construction.

Although quite small scale, one of the studies Chandler conducted with Dilwyn Roberts-Young involved interviews with Welsh adolescents about the meaning they attached to their personal homepages (Chandler and Roberts-Young, 1998).

Chandler and Roberts-Young assert:

> Not all personal homepages are overtly or primarily about their authors, but such pages do reveal their authors' interests to the reader ... One male seventeen-year-old told us that 'the purpose of the site is to advertise me ... The content reflects my interests, and therefore shows that user what kind of person I am ... All the content of the site reflects my personality'.
>
> (Chandler and Roberts-Young, 1998, p.2)

Citing the social psychologist Erik Erickson, Chandler and Roberts-Young remind us that the 'central question of adolescence is "Who am I?"' They contend that, 'the defining theme of personal homepages is this same question'. Moreover, they suggest, 'As a genre, the personal homepage seems well-adapted as a tool for this key task of adolescence, though clearly the use of the genre and the medium by teenagers is subject to both access and computer literacy' (Chandler and Roberts-Young, 1998, p.2).

In terms of form and content, the interviews with teenagers revealed an ability to draw upon a range of topics, media and other cultural resources. Chandler and Roberts-Young report that 'borrowing' is often a creative activity, citing the homepage of one of their subjects who 'appropriated and recontextualised the Smurf cartoon in a simple animated spoof of his own which he titled Smurfs and Away – "a protest against all soaps"' (Chandler and Roberts-Young, 1998, p.7).

This study and others by Chandler suggests that material is 'borrowed' rather extensively from other people's web pages. Corporate sites are pillaged too. As Chandler and Roberts-Young (1998, p.7) point out, 'the adoption of existing materials is much easier in virtual reality than in material reality, since virtual *bricolage* allows appropriation without either purchase or theft'.

Chandler and Roberts-Young raise another point: web pages are frequently revised. Citing a US survey, they report that 'in 1996 ... 63 per cent of personal webpage authors reported updating their pages at least once a month, and 25 per cent at least once a week'. This also reflects young people's desire to represent their changing maturity. One interviewee noted of her web page: 'I was happy with it when I first developed the site, but I would like to change it so that the pages are not so "young"' (Chandler and Roberts-Young, 1998, p.10).

This sense of being able to 'rewrite the self' supports what Chandler and Roberts-Young (1998, p.10) identify as the 'the post-modernist notion of [the self's] ... fluidity'. This area of interest has been developed in research on people's use of MUDs (multi-user domains) where different characters or roles are adopted by users.

One of the most compelling research reports on identity and the Internet is that of the social psychologist Sherry Turkle (1996b). Turkle takes up the analysis of the postmodern theorist Jean Baudrillard, arguing that there has been a collapse of distinctions between the 'real' and the 'virtual' through the proliferation of cultural representations that have formed **'hyper-realities'** constructed from simulacra (in short, representations that come to stand in for and ultimately absorb reality). For Turkle, this is exemplified par excellence by the Internet which offers new virtual opportunities and diverse identities. Turkle focuses on multi-user domains which she sees as 'neighbourhoods in cyberspace':

> MUDs, which originally stood for 'multi-user dungeons,' are destinations on the Internet where players who have logged in from computers around the world join an on-line virtual community. Through typed commands, they can converse privately or in large groups, creating and playing characters ... In many MUDs, players help build the virtual world itself.
>
> (Turkle, 1996a, p.1)

Turkle sees MUDs as offering opportunities for developing and exploring identities. At the same time, she is aware that these cyber-identities may not replicate the sensuous physical or emotional depth of face-to-face social and personal relationships. While providing opportunities for experiment, cyber-interaction may lend itself to identity confusion and crisis, or the virtual world may come to be a safe haven from the challenges of living in society. This is an issue raised in the film *The Matrix*, in which a small band of dissidents, aware that everyday life is a simulacra created by alien forms, confront a grim struggle in the 'real' and 'virtual' worlds. The character that betrays the dissidents does so in exchange for being returned to ignorance in the virtual world to enjoy its pleasures. In interviews with MUD users, Turkle discovered a similar recurring theme. For the young people Turkle interviewed, '"RL" (real life) was a place of economic insecurity where they had trouble finding meaningful work and holding on to middle-class status. Socially speaking, there was nowhere to go but down in RL, whereas MUDs offered a kind of virtual social mobility' (Turkle, 1996a, p.5).

This social mobility may also extend to taking on seemingly radical virtual identities. Turkle refers to representing oneself as of another gender, of indeterminate gender, or as an animal, not as subterfuge for deceitful

Hyper-reality
Baudrillard's concept which describes the extent to which 'reality' has been supplanted with a highly mediated reality, to the extent that 'reality' has lost all meaning – significance lies now only in representations.

communication, but an exploration of these different identities. These roles are not simply costumes worn or removed by the player. They constitute part of the identity of the player, but could not be achieved and experienced in the same way, or as authentically, through other than virtual representation in MUDs.

Sceptical that the 'virtual' should be seen as equivalent to the 'real', Kevin Robins (1995) argues:

> Through the development of new technologies, we are, indeed, more and more open to experiences of de-realisation and delocalisation. But we continue to have physical and localised existences. We must consider our state of suspension between these conditions. We must demythologise virtual culture if we are to assess the serious implications it has for our personal and collective lives.
>
> (Robins, 1995, p.153)

Robins argues for a sociology of cyberspace, supplanting what he regards as a utopian mythology. He urges greater application of social science methods to explore the meanings behind Internet use, instead of 'face-value' readings of its products. This is a critical point that can be brought against, for instance, Cheung's homepage research cited above.

Both Turkle's and Chandler and Roberts-Young's methods rely on interviews, but the two studies involve different approaches to the interview. Chandler and Roberts-Young's work involved semi-structured interviews with a small sample (26) of homepage producers. The sample was skewed in terms of gender, with 19 males and only 7 females. Interviews were conducted by e-mail, and though discussion was sought over a period of time, immersion in the field was necessarily limited. By contrast, Turkle's work is more ethnographic. By this she means extensive participant observation at online sites where people interface with computers and on MUDs themselves. In addition, Turkle sees her research as relying on 'clinical methods', reflecting her training in psychoanalysis, and involving interviews with MUD participants over a period of time to probe how virtual identities were constructed both consciously and sub-consciously.

The e-mail interviews Chandler and Roberts-Young and Turkle conducted raise interesting questions regarding the reliability and validity of their findings. Turkle muses at this new challenge to the researcher, 'what to make of on-line interviews and, indeed, whether and how to use them' (Turkle, 1996b, p.324). Immersed in the world of cyberspace, Turkle ascribes deep meaning to identity formation and play in MUDs. Chandler and Roberts-Young make similar claims for the activities of homepage producers. But at what level do those playing in MUDs or devising homepages conceptualize their activity? Turkle seems to have gathered her data from more committed MUD participants, so her analyses may not extend to transient or recreational MUDders who simply follow the narrative of a game, or who use forms of Internet technology for more conventional communication and interchanges. This raises a further question about the representativeness of her sample which relates to the validity and reliability of her analysis outside of self-identifying 'deep' MUDders. A similar concern might be raised regarding Chandler and Roberts-Young's sample of adolescent homepage producers.

Despite the limitations of Turkle's, Chandler and Roberts-Young's and Cheung's research, there are valuable ideas developed in their work. Qualitative methods provide the means to identify and explore frameworks of meaning. Against the richness of these insights are the perennial limitations to qualitative methods:

- the location of the researcher in the texts researched

- the tension between data and the theoretical frameworks that organize the data

- the limits of social science in providing analyses that might be coherent in their argument, comprehensive in their reach, reliable in their replication and valid in their assertion.

A review of web identities and the virtual communities of cyberspace offers new opportunities and problems for social researchers. For Turkle and others, research into MUDs and 'Internet identities' is partly a response to prevailing concerns regarding the 'anti-social' nature of online immersion. In contesting these wider assumptions, part of their project is to provide a critical perspective using the reasoned arguments and methods of social science. The sociologist David Hakken (1999) concludes his ethnography of cyberspace by noting that engaging in cyber-research not only introduces a rich new vocabulary of concepts that stimulate discussion and critique, but also allows the opportunity to go beyond describing and explaining cyberspace to having a role in shaping these new virtual worlds.

SUMMARY

- It is useful to distinguish between 'form' and 'content' when investigating representations.

- Understanding the use of different genre conventions can provide insights into the way meaning is produced.

- What we conventionally understand by 'identity' may be challenged by the opportunities allowed by the web.

- Research into web identities suggests that identities are increasingly 'fleeting' and 'hybridized'.

- Websites and other 'new media' are increasingly hybridized – often characterized by cross-genre forms.

- Some theorists (e.g. Baudrillard) suggest there is a notable collapse between the 'real' and the 'virtual', with the virtual offering new opportunities for identity construction.

- Different research interests need different methods. Textual analysis may tell us something about representations and culture, but to understand what meanings people make of their culture we must ask, or try to experience it with them.

5   CONCLUSION

In this chapter we have considered three studies concerned with identity, representation and culture and the role of ICTs in the information society. Each study yielded certain insights, but none provided definitive answers. Such is the nature of social science research. In addition, some tools and methods for analysing representations and their meanings for producers have been introduced. These methods, such as textual analysis or online interviews, despite their limitations, help develop deeper understandings of the contemporary world and its meanings. There is an important caveat, however. The usefulness of social science studies and methods rests upon their validity, reliability, comprehensiveness and coherence. For these particular studies, given the qualitative nature of most of the data collected and analyses executed, the prime criterion is *coherence*: logic and plausibility. Other criteria should not, however, be ignored: if a study cannot demonstrate a high degree of comprehensiveness, we may value it for specificity and depth, but we must acknowledge that it may be unlikely to yield wider insights.

We have explored studies of contemporary representations, the discourse of modernity tied up with new technology, identities which criss-cross established cultural boundaries, the availability of homepages and the possibilities for perpetually re-writing the self, and the significance of virtual communities such as MUDs for self-expression that side-steps some of the constraints of real life. Taken collectively, these constitute new and exciting areas for investigation. Certainly there are new subjects for empirical research (homepages, MUDs, virtual identities). There are also new issues (the cultural significance of virtuality, or the construction and re-writing of hybrid identities). For social scientists, these subjects, issues and their contexts additionally indicate a need for new methods of research (such as the online interview), and new forms of involvement in the fields of investigation.

New patterns of work and inequality

Hugh Mackay

1 INTRODUCTION

The second core theme of information society debates relates to work and inequality. Over the course of human history there has been a succession of technological developments which have transformed work. The industrial revolution and the establishment of the factory system was a major watershed, but in the contemporary era ICTs are transforming the quantity, quality and location of work across the breadth of sectors of the economy, and at a speed and scale which is probably unprecedented. They are changing the nature of work, the occupational structure, the skills of the workforce, control of the work process, the power and nature of management, and the gender composition of the workforce. This restructuring of work has led to new patterns of income and wealth distribution, of material inequality.

In Chapter 1 we discussed the decline of Fordism and its replacement by post-Fordist forms of organization, and in Chapter 2 we explored Daniel Bell's account of de-industrialization – the decline of manufacturing and the rise of the service or information sector. In this chapter we update and extend Bell's work. We start (in Section 2) by considering statistics on changes in work since 1970 which will enable us to consider whether the trends identified by Bell have continued, and how the occupational and economic structure has changed in the closing decades of the twentieth century.

This structural situation is important, but is not the only way in which we can explore the transformation of work and the economy. As well as the quantity of work, there have been profound changes in the *quality* of work, which we shall explore in Section 3. Quality of work, or job satisfaction, is important for a variety of reasons, complementing remuneration and status as measures of the worth of a given job. Exploring the quality of

Deskilling
Deskilling is a concept used in debates about the labour process. It concerns the relative power of management and workers in the control of work.

work, and changes to this with the transformation of the economy, involves considering the **deskilling** debate – the focus of much research on the labour process. The deskilling debate addresses whether and how the introduction of new technologies at work changes skill requirements and the power and control of workers and managers in relation to the labour process.

The main way in which contemporary transformations of the economy are conceived today is in terms of the emergence or growth of the 'e-economy', which is explored in Section 4. This is a term which carries a diversity of meanings, including new products, new organizations and, crucially, new means of delivery. These challenge the rules and conventions of economic organization, notably by changing dramatically the links between producers and consumers.

In Section 5 we explore the outcome of these processes – who are the winners, and who are the losers. We examine 'information haves' and 'have-nots' in terms of the UK and worldwide. We conclude, in Section 6, by considering some of the implications of these new ICTs and new inequalities for democracy.

2   BELL AND AFTER

As we saw in Chapter 2, Daniel Bell's work, and much of the information society debate, is rooted in an analysis of the restructuring of the economy – the shift from a predominantly manufacturing economy to one that is mainly a service and information economy.

ACTIVITY 6.1

Turn back to the discussion of Bell's work in Chapter 2, Section 2, to remind yourself of the main contours of Bell's arguments.

De-industrialization and the transformation to an information economy are generally understood by recourse to quantitative data. As we saw in Chapter 2, Bell's analysis is dependent on the quantitative data of the economists Machlup and Porat, who generated their data in the 1950s and 1960s. So how have things changed since then? Table 6.1 shows the volume and distribution across occupations of employment in the UK from 1971 to (projections for) 2009. They are *longitudinal* data, that is relating to the same category or phenomena over a period of time. Table 6.2 provides data for the same period on the distribution of employment across each category of industry.

TABLE 6.1   Employment trends by occupational group, 1971–98 and projections for 2009, UK

	1971	1981	1991	1998	2009
Total employment (millions)	24.4	24.5	26.0	27.1	29.4
	Per cent of total employment				
1 Managers and senior officials	11	10	13	13	13
2 Professional occupations	7	8	9	11	13
3 Associate professional and technical occupations	9	9	11	12	14
4 Administrative, clerical and secretarial occupations	14	16	16	15	14
5 Skilled trade occupations	19	17	15	14	12
6 Personal service occupations	3	4	5	6	7
7 Sales and customer service occupations	5	6	6	7	7
8 Process, plant and machine operatives	14	12	10	9	8
9 Elementary occupations	17	18	15	14	12
All occupations	100	100	100	100	100

Source: Department of Trade and Industry, 2000, Table 3.1, p.37

TABLE 6.2   Employment by industry, 1971–98 and projections for 2009, UK

	1971	1981	1991	1998	2009
Total employment (millions)	24.4	24.5	26.0	27.1	29.4
	Per cent of total employment				
Primary and utilities	7	6	4	3	2
Manufacturing	32	25	18	16	13
Construction	7	6	7	7	6
Distribution, transport, etc.	26	27	28	28	28
Business and miscellaneous services	12	15	20	24	29
Non-market services	18	21	23	23	22
All industries	100	100	100	100	100

Source: Department of Trade and Industry, 2000, Table 3.2, p.37

ACTIVITY 6.2

In relation to *each row* of Tables 6.1 and 6.2, note the trend over the period 1971–2009. For example, in the second row of Table 6.1 we can see that whereas in 1971 11% of the workforce of the UK consisted of managers and senior officials, it is projected that by 2009 this will be 13% (and of a workforce which has increased from 24.4 million to 29.4 million). Regarding each row, does what you have noted confirm or contradict Bell's thesis?

Bell's focus was on the USA and his argument was about the advanced industrial economies – a category which may be less clearly definable 30 years after his work, with economic globalization and the shift of manufacturing to areas with low labour costs. (Having said that, the shift of manufacturing to South-East Asia, and especially China, reflects precisely the decline of manufacturing in the West that Bell identified.) So it is interesting to explore – rather than the overall, almost uni-dimensional picture that Bell paints – the differences which exist between and within different industrialized countries. This can be examined by drawing on comparative studies of different countries and regions using official statistics which have been collected according to international standard classifications. Such data are collected by a number of official bodies, notably the Organization for Economic Cooperation and Development (OECD) and the International Labour Office (ILO). Much of these bodies' data and reports are available online, at www.oecd.org and www.ilo.org, and Table 6.3 shows OECD data on employment in the agricultural, industrial and service sectors between 1973 and 1993. Unlike the more numerous categories used in Tables 6.1 and 6.2, this uses data that have been agglomerated into something like Bell's three categories – agricultural, industrial and service – and represents these as **percentages**.

Percentages
A percentage is a fraction expressed as a proportion of 100.

TABLE 6.3 Percentage of labour force per sector in selected countries, 1973–93

	1973			1983			1993		
	Agric.	Ind.	Service	Agric.	Ind.	Service	Agric.	Ind.	Service
UK	2.9	42.4	54.6	2.7	33.6	63.8	2.2	26.2	71.6
USA	4.2	33.2	62.6	3.5	28.0	68.5	2.7	24.1	73.2
Spain	24.3	36.7	38.9	18.0	33.5	48.4	10.1	30.7	59.2
France	11.3	39.5	49.3	8.0	33.8	58.2	5.1	27.7	67.2
Germany	7.3	47.5	45.2	5.6	42.0	52.2	3.0	37.0	60.0

Source: OECD, 1994, cited in Duff and McCleery, 1996, p.162

ACTIVITY 6.3

Analyse the data in Table 6.3. Does each country display the trends identified by Bell? If so, to what degree (compared with other countries)? Can you think of any reasons for the differences between countries?

C O M M E N T _____

In every country we can identify a decline in the proportion of employment in agriculture and industry, and a rise in the proportion of the workforce in service employment, in the period 1973–93. There are, however, large variations between countries, with the proportion in agriculture in the UK roughly constant over these years, whilst the equivalent figure for other European countries is more than a halving. Spain, in particular, has seen much more dramatic change than the USA. The proportion in industrial employment in Spain has remained roughly constant, so it looks as if the growth of service employment there has not been at the expense of industrial employment – rather contradicting Bell. Data for the USA show that the proportion employed in service occupations has not risen much during the period. There are no data in the table to explain these changes, but we might conjecture or hypothesize that the shift from an industrial to a service economy took place earlier in the USA.

This activity involved examining percentages to make sense of longitudinal change, and they seem a useful way of representing and understanding the social change identified by Bell. Raw data, however, can be much more useful. Table 6.4 provides data on the number of jobs in each of the three categories of economic activity (primary, secondary and tertiary), in 1998, in selected countries.

TABLE 6.4   Employment by economic activity per three sectors, 1998 (thousands)

	Primary	Secondary	Tertiary	Total[1]
Canada	3,753.7	5,744.2	4,824.1	14,326.4
Denmark	99.86	1,081.70	1,509.74	2,692.37
Germany	1,206	17,103	17,515	35,860
Ireland	141.1	640.1	711.3	1,494.4
Spain	1,120.3	6,134.7	5,946.8	13,204.9
UK	564.8	11,178.8	15,110.7	26,947.4
USA	4,129	30,747	96,587	131,463

[1]Total employment is slightly higher than the sum of employment in each of the three sectors due to a small number of jobs being unclassified.

Source: International Labour Office, 1999, Table B

The data in Table 6.4 are amenable to much more processing and analysis than the percentage tables we have explored. In particular, they enable us to explore distribution, the spread of any variable across our cases. In the last column of Table 6.4 the variable is the total number of jobs – it is a feature that varies across the different cases, in this example, countries. Often it is useful to define a typical case, or country. Statistically, this can be done in several ways. The **median** is the mid point, the case which has an equal number of cases above as below it – which is a fair way of measuring typicality. The median is one way of representing the distribution of a variable (in our example, the total number of jobs) across cases (in our example, countries). Let's look at Table 6.4 and the column which shows employment in the primary sector. If we list the countries in ascending order, we can see that their employment in the primary sector is as shown in Table 6.5.

Median

The median is an average. It is the case which has the same number of cases above as below it. (If there is an even number of cases, the median is half way between the two middle cases.)

TABLE 6.5 Employment in the primary sector, 1998 (thousands)

Denmark	99.86
Ireland	141.1
UK	564.8
Spain	1,120.3
Germany	1,206
Canada	3,753.7
USA	4,129

Spain is the case, or country, with an equal number of countries above and below it, so it is the median.

ACTIVITY 6.4

Which is the median country in the last column of Table 6.4 – the country with an equal number of countries above as below it in terms of total number of jobs?

COMMENT

If you have any difficulties with this, re-read the paragraph before Table 6.5 above.

Mean

The mean is an average. It is calculated by adding the values of each case and dividing by the number of cases.

The most common way of finding the middle of a distribution, however, is the arithmetic **mean**, which is what is commonly referred to as the average. Unlike the median, the mean is determined by not just the number of cases above or below it, but by the scale of each case. To calculate the mean, add the figure for each case and divide by the number of cases. The case nearest to the answer is the mean case. Unlike the median, the mean is affected by cases that are particularly high or low.

ACTIVITY 6.5

Calculate from Table 6.4 (final column) the mean number of total jobs. Add the figures in the final column and divide by 7, the number of cases, or countries.

COMMENT _____

As your calculation should show, this identifies a different figure and a different country nearest the mean than the median case (or country). This is because, unlike the median, the mean takes account of the values of all of the data, including the extremities. So the case of the USA plays a significant part in making the mean higher than the median.

_____

In itself, neither median nor mean tell us anything about the spread of data in the column. Often it is useful to explore the spread of cases. This might be done by examining the *range*, the distance between the two extreme values. The **standard deviation** calculates the *typical* distance of each case from the mean. The standard deviation for the final column of Table 6.4 can be established by calculating each case's (country's) difference from the mean – 32,284, I made it. The UK, at 26,947.4, is 5,336.6 below the mean (32,284–26,947.4) and Germany is 3,576 (35,860–32,284) above it. The standard deviation is calculated by squaring each of these differences, adding these together, dividing the total by the number of cases minus 1, and calculating the square-root of this figure. The mathematics need not worry you, but the lower the standard deviation, the more clustered are the data around the mean. The standard deviation is useful because it tells us something about the distribution from the mean – whether cases are clustered close to the mean, or diverge from it widely. It is useful because in a distribution, 99 per cent of cases will normally be within three times the standard deviation of the mean.

Standard deviation
Standard deviation is a measure of the degree of dispersion of data.

Using statistical tests we can analyse quantitative data in a whole host of ways. However, our statistics are only as good as the data with which we are working. We have been looking at official statistics, collected by governments. These are useful for governments, but also for social scientists – Castells, as we saw in Chapter 2, roots his argument very much in official statistics. They tend to be regarded as particularly authoritative and objective. Commonly they are collected by large population surveys: the UK decennial census, for example, is a 100 per cent survey – it gathers data on standard questions from the entire population.

ACTIVITY 6.6

Refer back to Chapter 3, Section 2, where we define and discuss validity and reliability. Note any limits you can think of regarding the validity or reliability of official statistics.

C O M M E N T _____

Official statistics appear authoritative, but they are a representation of society, using preconceived categories, so they are subject to the usual problems of questionnaire surveys and positivist methodologies which we discussed in Chapter 4. More than this, we can question their validity as a measure. Unemployment figures, for example, are based on official returns from those registered for particular benefits and 'available for work'. It ignores those who, for various reasons, are not 'signing on'. At least one decennial census found about double the number of people claiming to be unemployed as was suggested by government unemployment figures at the same time, demonstrating very different definitions or classifications. Administrative or political decisions about benefits can have a huge impact on such data – which is produced by administrative systems which exist for other purposes. For instance, state bureaucracies are there to deliver services, not to collect official statistics. The latter are a by-product, not a primary function or aim of the organization.

In other ways, social processes shape social statistics. Here are two examples. The first is how tax rules affect wealth: data on the ownership of wealth is subject to the elderly wealthy donating their assets in accord with the tax system to avoid estate ('death') duty. The second is that all surveys have non-respondents, and these generally differ from those who respond to surveys. Thus social factors shape official statistics, rather than these being simply an objective measure of some reality. So, although they provide a vast amount of interesting figures and offer a depth of information that no researcher could amass on their own, official statistics are only as good as the quality of the data on which they are based.

3 DESKILLING AND THE QUALITY OF WORK

So far we have touched on the *quantity* of work. But as important is the experience, or *quality*, of work. We discussed Fordism in Chapter 1, which is based on Taylor's scientific management. F.W. Taylor applied engineering principles to the organization of work in the early decades of the twentieth century. His scientific management is rooted in breaking down every task into the smallest component possible, maximizing the division of labour (having different people doing different jobs) and developing a high level of control and coordination. Taylor's view – and he was enormously influential throughout the industrialized world, East and West – was that minimizing skill optimized productivity, a situation in which workers and managers had a mutual interest. With Taylorist principles and production-line technology, Henry Ford employed agricultural workers to mass-produce cars.

The deskilling thesis is associated with the author of *Labor and Monopoly Capital: The Degradation of Work in the Twentieth Century*, Harry Braverman, a former craft worker in the copper industry (Braverman, 1974). Braverman made a major contribution to the development of the deskilling thesis, arguing that reducing the skill level of a job reduces the cost of labour, so increases profitability. He and others argue that it is unsurprising that a succession of technologies have had the effect of reducing the skill levels of so many occupations, replacing the craft knowledge of workers with machines and lower-skilled labour. In the process, managerial control is extended, wages are reduced, and profitability is increased. An example that is often cited is the demise of the toolmaker with the rise of CNC (computer numerically controlled) machine tools. Machine tools lie at the heart of the engineering industry. Workers – many of them in the West Midlands of England – might calculate the depth to which a hole was drilled by taking account of the wear on a drill bit as it undertook its task. They would make calculations, perhaps on the back of a packet of Woodbines, which involved a tacit understanding of coefficients of expansion and other variables. CNC machine tools, by contrast, might only require the worker to attach and align the material to be processed, with the necessary calculations made automatically from digital drawings. Across many occupations a process of deskilling can be identified – for example, the reduced discretion and narrower breadth of tasks performed by workers in banking and insurance. Even regarding professional occupations there is discussion of 'proletarianization', with the autonomy of professionals constrained by a growing plethora of managerial controls. For example, not long ago, university lecturers were employed simply to research and teach in the area of their subject expertise. Today, in addition, they are subject to a range of monitoring, recording and evaluation mechanisms, notably teaching quality audits and the research assessment exercise. In such ways, they are subject to greater bureaucratic and managerial controls.

At the same time, with new technologies, new skills are required at work. Contemporary telecommunications and computing technologies entail some highly skilled work – often not in their operation, but certainly in their design, and commonly in their maintenance, too. Moreover, the skill of an operative might be extended by reducing the division of labour, for instance, having one worker looking after more machines, or a maintenance worker covering both electrical and mechanical, for example.

Skill is not easy to measure, and is commonly confused with manual dexterity. It is perhaps best measured by length of time in training. On this basis, a brain surgeon is more highly skilled than a bus conductor, and at these extremes few would disagree. But this ignores the power – for example, of a professional association to control the training process – to maintain the exclusivity, and thus remuneration, of a particular occupation. 'Length of training' has other limitations as a measure of skill because of background skills – GCSE mathematics was the example we mentioned in Chapter 2. According to Braverman, skill is defined in terms of the degree of worker control of the work process, with a craft worker highly skilled and an operative on a production line with a two-minute cycle time (performing the same task every two minutes) much less skilled. This seems a helpful analysis, but it assumes that skill (and power at work) is a zero sum process; a fixed quantity is distributed in various possible ways, so that power is with managers or workers. The latter is a particular model of power at work, associated with a Marxist perspective, but is criticized by others who argue that it gives insufficient attention to workers' agency. Others argue that managers and workers can work together to mutual benefit, because productivity is enhanced by maximizing worker control and reducing managerial intervention and the bureaucracy with which that is associated. In the computer graphics or animation industries, for example, one finds little formal supervision and considerable flexibility in the conditions of work.

One important dimension of skill is the subjective: how it is seen by workers themselves. Whilst there's no obvious large-scale survey data on precisely this matter, some questions in the British Social Attitudes (BSA) survey on the subject of decision making at work are fairly close. For our purposes, we can use such questions to explore perceptions of control at work, as something of a substitute or *surrogate* for data on the precise subject of our concern.

We might expect decision-making processes to differ between types of job or types of workplace. So we can formulate a research hypothesis, such that the **dependent variable** is 'attitude to decision making in work', and the **independent variables** are occupational sector (regarding which the BSA survey can be used to distinguish between private and public sectors) and mode of work (regarding which the BSA has data on full- or part-time work). Thus we can use large-scale government survey data to explore a hypothesis regarding perceptions of control at work.

The first stage in exploring a set of data such as the BSA survey is to scan the data looking for suitable variables that might throw some light on a research hypothesis. Since we are engaged in **secondary analysis** it is unlikely that the concerns of the original researcher will be exactly the same as ours. Nonetheless, before engaging in expensive and time consuming **primary research**, it is always well worth checking to see if somebody else has collected data that we can use.

In Table 6.6 we produce a simple **cross-tabulation** to begin to explore variables relating to the hypothesis that attitudes to decision making in work are affected by occupational sector. Using a hypothesis that links them, we can explore possible connections between two variables. Table 6.6 is generated in SPSS, the Statistical Package for the Social Sciences.

Dependent variable
The dependent variable is the phenomenon we are concerned to explain.

Independent variables
Independent variables are those that we feel are likely to have an effect on the dependent variable.

Secondary analysis
Secondary analysis is analysis of data collected by other researchers.

Primary research
Primary research involves gathering one's own data.

Cross-tabulation
Cross-tabulations or contingency tables are tables in which the independent variable is placed in a column and the dependent variable in a row. Numbers in the cells are the number or percentage of cases with the characteristics of the column and the row.

TABLE 6.6   Cross-tabulation of how much say the respondent has in their work by occupational status (public or private)

| | | | Occupational sector | | |
			1 Private sector	2 Public sector	Total
How much say respondent has at work	1 A great deal	Number	134	35	169
		%	24.0%	14.5%	21.2%
	2 Quite a lot	Number	231	96	327
		%	41.4%	39.8%	40.9%
	3 Just a little	Number	193	110	303
		%	34.6%	45.6%	37.9%
Total		Number	558	241	799
		%	100.0%	100.0%	100.0%

Source: British Social Attitudes, 1996, available from ESRC Data Archive, University of Essex

The BSA asked respondents how much say they have in their work. In Table 6.6 the dependent variable is in the rows, and the independent variable (here, occupational sector) is in the columns. The columns sum to 100, which indicates that we are using column percentages. The procedure for analysing such a table is very easy. We begin by *reading across each of the rows*, starting with the top row which asks how many and what percentage of respondents felt that they had a great deal of influence over decisions taken at work which might affect them. The final column gives us the total percentage from the entire sample who said that they thought they had a great deal of influence. It is always the percentage, rather than the actual number, that is used, because the percentage is standardized (out of 100) whereas the total numbers in each column vary. This figure, 21.2%, is the **benchmark**. If it were the case that there were no relationship between the variables we would expect the benchmark figure to be repeated across the row. In other words, we would expect 21.2% of those in the private sector and 21.2% of those in the public sector to say that they had a great deal of influence. To analyse the data all we need to do at this stage is to scan the row to see if there are any differences in the figures. Clearly there is, so even at this elementary stage we can suspect a relationship between sector (public or private) and influence at work, although we do not know the *strength* of this relationship.

At this point we can introduce some very simple statistics to our analysis. The simplest measure of **association** is a statistic called *Epsilon*. This is a simple mathematical statistic which subtracts the lowest percentage in the row (excluding the benchmark) from the highest. 24.0 (column 1) minus 14.5 (column 2) gives an Epsilon of 9.5. How strong is this? The beauty of Epsilon

Benchmark
A benchmark is a baseline figure from which variation can be measured.

Association
Association is a link between two variables.

is its simplicity and it does not take much knowledge of mathematics to realize that its range must be from 0 to 100, and the closer it is to 100 the stronger the relationship. As a general rule of thumb an Epsilon less than 25 is going to indicate a very weak relationship.

Correlation

Correlation is a measure of association. Variables correlate when, as one rises, the other either rises or falls.

Because Epsilon is so simple it is not a statistic on which any researcher would want to stake their reputation. Far more common is a measure of association called **correlation**. There are a number of measures of correlation, but the basic principle behind them is always the same. *Two variables correlate when, as one rises, the other either rises or falls.*

Correlations are always expressed as a number ranging from 0 to 1. Some measures of correlation also include a measure of direction (i.e. positive or negative correlation). There are several tests of correlation, and which is used depends on the nature of the data. In this case we have nominal and ordinal data. Nominal data means that the data are simply categories, with no implied order – for instance, the categories '1' and '2' in Table 6.6 relating to occupational sectors. Clearly, it does not really matter which order the categories appear in, and the numbers are purely descriptive and cannot be regarded as quantities. If they were quantities, or scale data, then one could work with them using the full range of mathematical functions. Ordinal data share many of the properties of nominal data, but in addition have an implied order. The rows in Table 6.6 contain such data, the categories 'A great deal', 'Quite a lot' and 'Just a little' have a clear implied order, and would not make logical sense in the 'wrong' order. However, the numbers '1', '2' and '3' are still purely descriptive and should not really be considered as mathematical quantities. With nominal and ordinal data an appropriate measure of correlation is Cramers V, which is used for anything larger than a 2 × 2 table.

Correlation coefficient

The correlation coefficient measures the strength of association between two variables.

The **correlation coefficient** measures the extent to which one variable relates to another. The correlation coefficient for Table 6.6 is 0.126, a figure much closer to zero than one, indicating a weak relationship. The mathematics of how this is calculated need not bother us: the calculation can be made by SPSS. Psychologists would find this a low level, whereas sociologists would see it as an indication of a moderate relationship. There is no hard and fast rule for what is regarded as a strong relationship, which depends very much on disciplinary traditions and the type of research you are engaged in. For most social scientists, a correlation coefficient of 0.1 and above would not be dismissed.

Statistical significance

Tests of statistical significance measure statistically the chance that results are random in their occurrence.

So, looking at Table 6.6, we have a sense that there is some relationship between the occupational sector (public or private) and perceptions of having a say in decision making at work, but not necessarily a very strong one. The question is: how **statistically significant** is the relationship? To answer the question we need to know about sampling. Statistical significance assumes that the data have been selected randomly, which is the case with the BSA survey. Most researchers are less concerned to say that their *sample* has *x* or *y* characteristic, but want to say something about the entire population from which the sample was drawn. This is usually expressed as a **probability ratio**. For example, we might say that we are confident within a 5 per cent parameter that the results can be generalized to the population as a whole.

One measure of statistical significance widely used in the social sciences is **chi square**. Chi square is calculated on the basis of the real (observed) figures in each of the cells in the table and those that would be *expected if there were no relationship* between the variables being tested. Through a series of computations, this information can be turned into a chi square figure and a probability ratio expressed. It is usual to accept as statistically significant anything with a probability of 0.05 or greater. This means that there are five chances in 100 that the results occurred by chance. Some clinical researchers, including some psychologists, rely on a probability ratio of 0.01, meaning a one in 100 chance of the results occurring by chance. The figure for the table reported above is 0.0001, a one in 10,000 chance of the result occurring by chance.

So there are many ways – and we have introduced only the basics – in which statistical techniques can be employed to understand social change and the transformation of work. They are important, in particular, for understanding the validity of data and of the claims that are made from them.

By deploying quantitative as well as qualitative analysis, researchers have found that new technologies can be introduced in ways that both increase and reduce skill, depending on the technology and the context. Managerial style and control are not a function or reflection of technology, but something which is exercised in a variety of ways. Skill is not a straightforward matter to measure, and is seen by many as encompassing an element of subjective perception – something that, as we have seen, can be explored using quantitative as well as qualitative data.

The new e-economy is characterized by a variety of organizational forms, work settings and power relations. Call centres, a major feature of the new economy, resemble closely the Fordist factory in many respects. Other parts of the new economy, including the multi-media industries, seem far-removed from Fordism. The journalist Anna Tobin has described her experience working for a dot.com startup company in 2000:

> An assortment of people decked out in a mixture of Prada, New Look and Firetrap clothes pile into the freshly painted lilac and lemon boardroom. There's hardly anyone over the age of 35. The early birds get the comfy chairs, the rest of the flock perch on the edge of the table. The old-timers – those who have served more than a fortnight – snigger as they measure up the newcomers and take bets on the bizarre ritual to which they are about to be subjected.

> The chief executive burst into the room and the twittering stops. He hands around a bag of ice lollies, introduces himself to the latest recruits and then asks: 'What's your name? Where do you come from? And when did you last have sex?' ...

Probability ratio
The probability ratio expresses the relative size of two variables, as in the bookie's 4–1.

Chi square
The chi square test is used commonly to explore the relationship between two variables. It compares observed figures with those one would expect normally, if there were no relationship between the two variables.

I have never considered myself eligible for Mensa prior to working at Talkcast, but all of a sudden I was being told that I was a genius at least once a week. I knew that everybody else's intellect was also being regularly showered with praise, but somehow it still made me feel special.

Some of the characters I met at Talkcast would have been accused of overacting if they'd appeared in *Attachments* [a BBC2 dot.com drama series].

(Tobin, 2000)

This illustrates aspects of the labour process associated with the new, or e-, economy, to which we shall now turn.

4   THE E-ECONOMY

The growth of a service economy identified by Bell coincides with something with which the service economy overlaps but should not be confused: the development of the e-economy. This is a loose term, used increasingly by the media, politicians and industrialists, to refer to electronic trading. New technologies, and particularly the Internet, are changing the economy. In particular, they offer possibilities for linking producers and service suppliers with consumers in ways which cut out wholesalers and retailers: online banking and car purchasing, for example. In the process, relationships between businesses and customers are changed. For example, the management consultants McKinsey found that 98.7 per cent of visitors to a website never return, regardless of whether or not they make a purchase (Hayward, 2000). As the Internet wreaks its transformations, it is argued, competition increases, work is transformed, the significance of place changes, time speeds up, and organizations become integrated or excluded – themes that Castells explores, as we saw in Chapter 2. There is at least a mythology that budding entrepreneurs can start global businesses from their bedrooms, as barriers to entry are lowered, and brand loyalty evaporates as consumers shop around for the cheapest source. Large numbers of organizations are developing an electronic presence, usually at a considerable loss, in order to insure for the future. Many are run by inexperienced entrepreneurs, so it is not surprising that they are even more prone to failure than other new small companies. At the time of writing, few websites in the UK are making money, yet venture capitalists appear to be falling over themselves in their rush to finance dot.com companies. Although the dot.com economy represents a tiny single figure percentage of market capitalization, it is receiving a remarkable level of publicity, as a glance at the business pages of a quality newspaper testifies, and despite the publicity given to lastminute.com and other dot.com crashes. So whilst one should be cautious, most commentators see major transformations as underway.

The e-economy is associated with greater fluidity of labour, with reduced company loyalty and increased job insecurity. The sociologist Richard Sennett argues that multiple careers and job insecurity are something of a defining characteristic of the contemporary era (Sennett, 1998). There is some evidence, however, that he is incorrect, in that they are much less prevalent than is suggested by his argument. Although many workers *feel* that their jobs are less secure, only in Spain and the USA has there been a clear decline in average job tenure, whilst this has increased in France, Japan, the Netherlands, Germany and elsewhere. Although in some sectors or occupations there is considerable fluidity, in many others this is not the case: there is a danger in generalizing from Silicon Valley-like occupations (Bowers and Martin, 2000). Whatever such empirical evidence, Sennett's ideas seem useful in that he links job insecurity with senses of self, identity and social worth.

5   WINNERS AND LOSERS

In these processes of technological, organizational and economic restructuring of work, there have been winners and losers. Patterns of inequality, of the distribution of income and wealth, have *not* remained constant in recent years, but nor are the changes that we might have expected.

Starting with wealth, in the UK the most wealthy 1% of the population shared between them about 19% of **marketable wealth** in 1996, a proportion which has declined just a little over the preceding 20 years. The distribution of marketable wealth is shown in Table 6.7.

Marketable wealth
Marketable wealth consists of assets that can be sold or cashed in, such as shares or dwellings.

TABLE 6.7   Distribution of marketable wealth, UK, 1976–96

Marketable wealth, percentage of wealth owned by:	1976	1981	1986	1991	1995	1996
			Percentages			
Most wealthy 1%	21	18	18	17	19	19
Most wealthy 5%	38	36	36	35	38	39
Most wealthy 10%	50	50	50	47	50	52
Most wealthy 25%	71	73	73	71	72	74
Most wealthy 50%	92	92	90	92	92	93
Total marketable wealth (£ billion)	280	565	955	1,711	1,965	2,042

Source: *Social Trends* 30, 2000, Table 5.25, p.97

Examine Table 6.7 and identify the percentage of marketable wealth owned by the *least* wealthy half of the population in 1996. How has this changed over 20 years?

C O M M E N T

The penultimate line, the one before the total, tells us that the most wealthy 50% of the population owned (in 1996) 93% of wealth. That row shows us that 20 years earlier the figure was almost identical (92%) – so the *least* wealthy 50% owns 7% of wealth.

Turning to income, we find a rather different trend. During the 1980s there was a huge increase in inequality in the distribution of household income, but this slowed down in the 1990s. Figure 6.1 shows this distribution between 1971 and 1997: the bottom 10% earn almost the same in 1997 as in 1971, whilst the top 10% earn in 1997 almost double what they did in 1971.

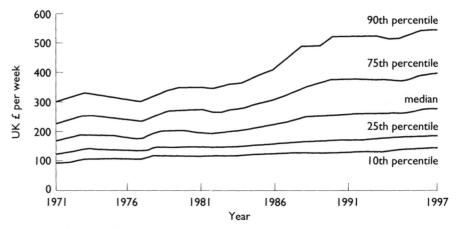

FIGURE 6.1   Distribution of real household disposable income, UK, 1971–97
Source: *Social Trends* 30, 2000, Chart 5.1, p.81

So official statistics show that – in terms of income – the rich are getting richer, whilst the poorest are not. Contemporary debates about social exclusion identify information as a key dimension of poverty, and digital exclusion as a problem. Online access is closely related to income: of households with a weekly income of £270 or less, which is the poorest third of households, only 3–6% (depending on their region of the UK) enjoy World Wide Web access, whereas nearly half of households with a weekly income of £900+ do so. There are powerful regional variations, with household online access in London and South-East England at 25%, in Northern Ireland 11%, and in Wales and Scotland about 15% (Kelso and Adams, 2000). In the USA, the rich are 20 times more likely to have Internet access than the poor (Lerner, 2000). The rich are likely to have access to higher bandwidth, hence cheaper and more accessible information. Such patterns can be seen as both cause and consequence of social exclusion. Without access to information, IT and IT skills, one is excluded from not just the dot.com economy and a breadth of new occupations, but from participation in society and politics. The Internet is a medium of expression as well as a source of information, hence a lack of computer literacy has been equated with not being able to read and write in the industrial era, the old economy.

In recognition of this situation, the UK government expresses consistently a firm commitment to extending IT access and Internet skills. The Chancellor of the Exchequer stated in his 1999 budget speech that 'anyone left out of the new knowledge revolution will be left behind in the new knowledge economy' (cited by Kelso and Adams, 2000), whilst Tony Blair has argued that the Internet must not remain the preserve of an elite, and that Britain must have an 'Internet for the people' (Ward, 2000). He has warned against 'a society divided into computer haves and have-nots' (cited in Kelso and Adams, 2000). At the time of writing, the government's UK Online Project aims to achieve universal access to the Internet by 2005 and online facilities in all schools and libraries by 2002. 700 special access centres are to open in deprived areas. By 2004, 75% of people living in deprived neighbourhoods will have the capabilities of access to electronically delivered public services, and 100% by 2008 (Department of Trade and Industry, 2000, p.59). The BBC News website is a useful source of information on a panoply of government measures in this field.

There are variations within countries and between advanced industrial countries but, globally, inequalities are much more stark. For Nelson Mandela, 'Eliminating the distinction between information-rich and information-poor countries is critical to eliminating the other inequalities between north and south' (cited in Atkinson, 2000). In a similar vein, Kofi Anan, UN Secretary General in 1999, has said:

> People lack many things: jobs, shelter, food, health care and drinkable water. Today, being cut off from basic telecommunications services is a hardship almost as acute as these other deprivations, and may indeed reduce the chances of finding remedies to them.
>
> (speech at Telecom 99, Geneva, October 1999, reported by BBC News Online, at http://news.bbc.co.uk/hi/english/special_report/1999/10/99/information_ rich_information_poor/newsid_466000/466651.stm#top, accessed 22 January 2001)

There is general agreement with this argument that access to information is an essential condition of development. But, at the same time as enabling the delivery of health care or education, ICTs are extremely expensive and consume the resources that could otherwise be going on medicine or teachers, for instance.

The disparity between rich and poor countries, in terms of ICTs, is dramatic (see Panos Communications and Social Change Programme, 1998). There are

1.5 telephone lines per 100 people in developing countries, and in Chad, Zaire and Cambodia, 1 per 1,000 people. 80 per cent of the population of Kenya lives in areas with no telephone, and the cost of a personal computer in Ethiopia is 15 times the per capita GDP.

> In Africa, for example, with 739m people, there are only 14m phone lines – fewer than in Manhattan – and 80% of those are in six countries ... While last year Britain had 15m internet subscribers, there were only 1m on the African continent. The average rich industrialised country has roughly 40 times the per capita number of computers of a sub-Saharan African country (excluding South Africa), 100 times as many mobile phones, and 1,600 times as many internet hosts.
>
> (Atkinson, 2000)

> An inhabitant of a high-income country is four times more likely to have access to a television set than an inhabitant of a low-income country; 25 times more likely to have access to a telephone; but almost 8,000 more likely to have access to an Internet host computer.
>
> (International Telecommunication Union, quoted in Panos Communications and Social Change Programme, 1998)

> The United States has more computers than the rest of the world combined. Bulgaria has more Internet hosts than the whole of sub-Saharan African, excluding South Africa. South Asia, with 23 per cent of the world's people, has less than one per cent of the world's Internet users ... The typical Internet user worldwide is male, under 35 years old, with a university education and high income, urban based and English speaking ... Yet fewer than one in 10 people worldwide speaks the language.
>
> (United Nations Development Programme, 1999)

Figure 6.2 shows the vast disparity between countries in use of the Internet.

Drawing a link between development and communication is nothing new, with the radio seen by many in the 1950s as a panacea. Today, radio covers about 75% of the African population, television 40% and the Internet 0.1%; so some argue that the way to development has to be via the radio. The Internet should not be a priority, it is argued, if there are hardly any telephones or, more dramatically, if there is no electricity: one in three people globally lack access to electricity. Others, however, claim that it might be possible for developing countries to bypass the industrial era, and that the Internet offers possibilities for achieving economic advantage.

Most early users of the Internet in developing countries were academics, community organizations and NGOs (non-governmental organizations). Thus

Most wired

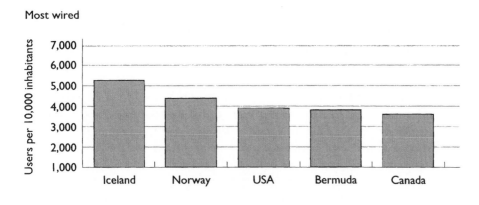

Least wired

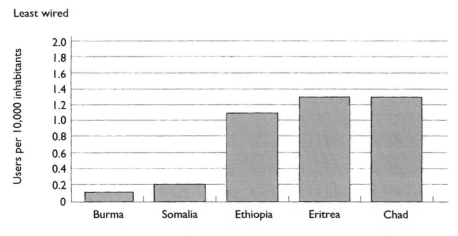

FIGURE 6.2   Use of the Internet per 10,000 inhabitants, selected countries
Source: BBC News Online, at http://news.bbc.co.uk/hi/english/sci/tech/newsid_843000/843160.stm (accessed 16 October 2000)

some of the best informed organizations in developing countries were those campaigning for greater democracy, social equality, and protection of the environment. The growth of the Internet, however, has been driven very much by commercial imperatives, and developing countries are often not viable, let alone profitable, for Internet connection. Whatever the pros and cons, there is a plethora of initiatives to introduce and extend use of the Internet in developing countries. For example, George Soros the international financier, has devoted millions of dollars to this in Eastern Europe through his Open Society Institute. The issue for him is not simply economic development but democracy, the theme on which we shall conclude this chapter.

6   INFORMATION EXCLUSION AND DEMOCRACY

The significance of the Internet for democracy is not an issue of concern only to developing countries. The development of ICTs is taking place in a context of deregulation of the media (e.g., in the UK, relaxing the amount of ITV that one company can own), privatization of state provision (e.g. of telecommunications) and the general growth of the liberal, free, market. Together these represent a significant shift for the media, and other organizations and institutions, from people being seen as citizens, towards being seen as consumers.

There are long-standing traditions of thought that link citizenship to communications. In the UK, rather like other industrialized nations, access to communications and information developed largely in the nineteenth century, with the provision of public libraries, state education and, later, public broadcasting. A part of the rationale for such developments was the notion that being a full member of society involves not simply participation in the political process, but access to information. The media sociologists Graham Murdock and Peter Golding argue that among the various dimensions of the communications–citizenship links is:

> access to the broadest possible range of information, interpretation, and debate on areas that involve political choices, and [citizens] must be able to use communications facilities in order to register criticism, mobilize opposition, and propose alternative courses of action.
>
> (Murdock and Golding, 1989, p.183)

This involves diversity of production and, on the consumption side, universal access. Their argument is that the market system can guarantee neither. 'Markets address people primarily in their role as consumers rather than citizens. Indeed, they present the freedom to choose among competing products as the central and defining liberty of the modern age' (Murdock and Golding, 1989, p.192).

This is a rather more sceptical, or measured, analysis than the techno-enthusiasm of much of the information society discourse, which we considered in Chapter 1. In technical terms, contemporary ICTs allow unlimited access to information, push-button democracy, voter juries, and a more participative, responsive, democracy. More than this, the Internet clearly circumvents the territorial sovereignty of nation-states, allowing global association, community and even citizenship (though quite what that means beyond the context of the nation-state seems unclear). Information can bypass state controls, decentralize production and distribution, and empower citizens. For the techno-utopian Howard Rheingold (whose ideas we shall discuss in Chapter 7) the Internet is the twenty-first century's version of the

Greek agora, eighteenth-century coffee houses, the village square or the street corner, providing a forum for the revitalization of community and democracy. Low cost, interactive, global access is profoundly democratizing. The reality of the development of ICTs, as we have seen, is rather different, with the commodification of information, the increasing concentration of economic power, and growing inequalities.

7   CONCLUSION

In this chapter we have reviewed some arguments and data regarding the transformation of work and changing patterns of inequality. In general, we have been exploring quantitative data, and we have introduced some statistical techniques for handling quantitative data. We have considered means, medians, standard deviations, correlations and tests of statistical significance. Generally, like Castells, we have been exploring official statistics, and we have considered their strengths (notably their scope, volume and availability) and limits (e.g. regarding their validity).

We began Chapter 2 by asserting that the work of Bell and Castells lies at the heart of information society debates. In this chapter we have explored and updated some of the issues raised by Bell, notably his thesis regarding de-industrialization and the growth of the service sector in industrialized societies. In Chapter 2 we explored some major difficulties involved in the classification of data regarding employment and the economy on which his argument is based. In this chapter we have rather suspended that judgement, and explored instead how the world has changed in the period since Bell's work and other ways in which recent developments are understood by social scientists.

In many ways the data sustain Bell's analysis regarding the growth of the tertiary sector. International comparison, however, shows the process to be very far from uniform. Crucially, the data can be interpreted in various ways. In Braverman's work on deskilling, and other work on which we have touched, the logic and consistency of argument is perhaps more important than the evidence which researchers have collected or drawn on. We have seen how different perspectives are brought to bear on the available data in leading to very different arguments.

We have argued that new technology is an important component in the contemporary restructuring of work. Whilst such a process is nothing new, the scale, speed, volume and global reach of the transformation of work seems important. In the process, there are winners and losers – with those with higher incomes in the UK earning very much more than they did 30 years ago, whilst the income of the poorest fractions of society has remained constant. This is a situation commonly characterized in terms of social polarization, and in this process, information, access to ICTs, and relevant knowledge and capability, are now seen as important. Within the UK and globally we can identify a series of policies that are aimed at providing access to ICTs and information. The rationale for these varies and is often linked to economic development. Information exclusion, however, is more important than this: access to information, and to a diversity of sources and analyses, is seen by many as a core component of citizenship.

We have seen how social science theories and concepts are drawn on in interpreting large-scale survey and other quantitative data, and in constructing arguments. We have also seen, in passing, the wealth of data that are available in various online sources, which are used increasingly by social researchers. As we shall see in the following chapter, the social science methods and sources we have examined in this chapter are complemented by others. Together, these are how social scientists make sense of the information society.

Time–space reconfiguration

chapter 7

Hugh Mackay

● ●

1 INTRODUCTION

The third core theme which we can identify in information society debates concerns changes in our conception and experience of both time and space – a theme we have explored in the work of Manuel Castells in Chapter 2. For a long while it has been acknowledged in social theory that time and space are closely linked: shortening dramatically the time that it takes to communicate with (or travel to) a distant place makes that place seem nearer, and we can't talk of space without a conception of time. It has also long been recognized that social life is routinized around time and space (Giddens, 1990). Because interaction takes place in time and space, and can't be understood without account of this, then *changes* in time or space are profoundly significant for society, but also for social theory. The historian Edward Thompson is among those who have discussed the significance of the clock, perhaps the defining symbol of the industrial era. Social life became regulated by factory hours, instead of by the weather, seasons or daylight (Thompson, 1967). Another social historian, Eric Hobsbawn, writing of the last quarter of the twentieth century as the 'economic, social and cultural transformation, the greatest, most rapid and most fundamental in recorded history', states that 'perhaps the most dramatic practical consequence ... was a revolution in transport and communication which virtually annihilated time and distance' (Hobsbawn, 1995, pp.8, 12, cited in Hakken, 1999).

The rate of speed-up can hardly be overstated. Take the example of the Holyhead to London mail route, which was (and is) used for travel to Ireland. Early in the nineteenth century the journey routinely took 40 hours. By 1830, following the introduction of mail coaches, this had been reduced to 27 hours, but it was nonetheless incredibly expensive, unreliable and dangerous. The semaphore telegraph, developed a little before the railways, meant that, for the first time, news could travel faster than a person on horseback or sail boat. The Holyhead telegraph, for example, consisted of a serious of towers, sited above the sea mist but below the mountain cloud, between Holyhead (on Anglesey) and Liverpool. When a ship arrived off Holyhead – and it might have been six weeks late or thought to have been lost at sea – messages about its state and cargo could be communicated, via a code, to agents and owners in Liverpool. The railway opened along the north Wales coast in 1848 and today the journey from Holyhead to London takes about 4 hours by rail with a service every couple of hours during the day.

So today is not the first time we can talk about the compression of time and distance. But the idea has really risen to prominence with the work of social theorists who argue that we are living in a late modern or postmodern era (Jameson, 1984; Soja, 1989). They accord a central place in their argument to the shrinking of space, the speed-up of time, and instantaneous electronic communication.

Electronic communication – and the almost limitless volume and instant speed with which information can be transmitted – underlies and enables the Internet and global coordination. Contemporary digital information networks lie at the core of information society debates. Different theorists discuss these in different ways. The sociologist Anthony Giddens refers to 'time–space distanciation' and 'time–space convergence', the cultural geographer David Harvey talks of 'time–space compression' and Castells, as we explored in Chapter 2, refers to a shift from the 'space of place' to the 'space of flows' (Giddens, 1990, 1984; Harvey, 1990; Castells, 1996). By focusing on networks and connections, we shall be examining the contributions of geographers to the information society discourse. The concerns of geographers with place complement the work of sociologists and economists which we've examined.

The core of the issue is that a series of social and technological changes have transformed earlier spatial and temporal arrangements and constraints. Connection today has changed, as is illustrated by work on the visualization and analysis of Internet traffic. Figure 7.1 is an example of this work.

ACTIVITY 7.1

What does Figure 7.1 (opposite) tell us about time–space aspects of communication? (If you have access to the Internet, you may like to consult this and other spatial representations of cyberspace in a remarkable collection at the *Atlas of Cyberspace* site, http://www.cybergeography.org/atlas/atlas.html)

COMMENT

This map shows clearly the domination of the Internet by North America, in particular, and Europe. Having said that, Australia, New Zealand and parts of South America also seem well-connected. Thinking back to Castells' work on networks, we can see how connection transcends time and space.

Such representations of levels of usage, however, tell us nothing about who is using the technology or for what purpose. Figure 7.1 doesn't tell us how the

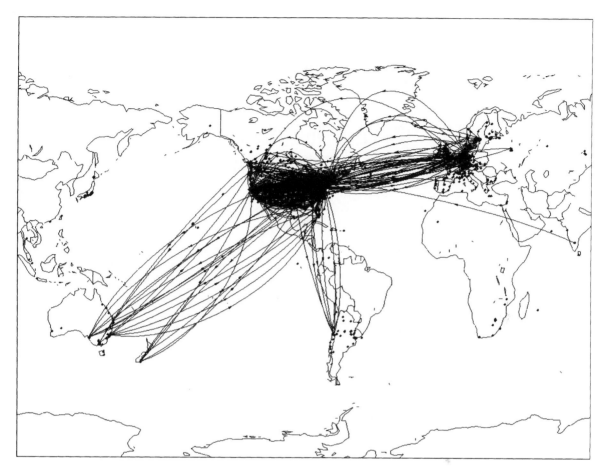

FIGURE 7.1 Eick's visualization and analysis of Internet traffic
Source: http://www.cybergeography.org/atlas/geographic.html

technology intersects with everyday life. We argued in Chapter 2 that both a strength and a weakness of Castells' work is its wide range, the all-encompassing scope of his analysis. On the positive side, this means that he has taken account of Asia, Africa, Japan and so on in his data collection and analysis – his is by no means a US- or Europe-centric account. But a weakness, you may recall, is that his core concept, the network, remains ill-defined. In other words, Castells' account, following his theoretical predispositions, is rooted in grand or macro analysis. He certainly relates the broad canvas he paints to specific local conditions: the poor of Columbia, for example. Such examples, deployed to illustrate and bring to life his broader argument, are congruent with his argument. To explore the validity of his claims thoroughly, however, we would have to go further, to explore local settings to see if they confirm or refute his theory.

To complement his macro view, we shall examine two research projects that focus on specific instances of time–space transformation: Internet communities and an example of a new media technology, satellite television in its early days in the UK. As we examine the two research projects we shall develop the substantive area of time–space reconfiguration; evaluate each project in terms of its validity, reliability, comprehensiveness and coherence; and discuss the principles and practice of the methods which are used.

2 INTERNET COMMUNITIES: AN INTRODUCTION

The first area of research addressing time–space reconfiguration which we'll explore is Internet communities.

> After three thousand years of explosion, by means of fragmentary and mechanical technologies, the Western world is imploding. During the mechanical ages we had extended our bodies in space. Today, after more than a century of electric technology, we have extended our central nervous system itself in a global embrace, abolishing both time and space as far as our planet is concerned. Rapidly, we approach the final phase of the extensions of man – the technological simulation of consciousness, when the creative process of knowing will be collectively and corporately extended to the whole human society, much as we have already extended our senses and our nerves by the various media.
>
> (McLuhan, 1964, p.11)

Perhaps surprisingly, this is how Marshall McLuhan opens *Understanding Media* in 1964. His ideas, notably regarding the 'global village', are facing something of a revival with the development of the Internet.

Today, Internet communities offer for some the possibility of realizing McLuhan's notion. Those involved enjoy instant, global communication and communities are freed from the constraint of place which has been a key characteristic of pre-Internet communities. The Internet extends the space available for communication and interaction.

There is a plethora of research that sees computer-mediated communication (CMC) via the Internet as fostering a sense of community, involving shared, close and intimate interaction. In allowing new modes of interaction and networks it allows new forms of social relationship which lack the constraints of time and space. With the facility of many-to-many communication, global reach and instant transmission, it allows views to be expressed, ideas shared and thoughts developed, requiring neither spatial nor temporal co-presence. Steven Jones, a Professor of Communication in the USA, argues that this isn't just supporting new social relations but is producing a different kind of society (Jones, 1995).

Howard Rheingold is one of the most often cited proponents of the new communities which are enabled by the Internet. His analysis is rooted in the demise of community in the USA, and he sees Internet communities as overcoming or reversing trends towards social disintegration, although, this time, on a global scale, freed from the constraints of physical, geographical boundaries and distance.

> I suspect that one of the explanations for this phenomenon is the hunger for community that grows in the breasts of people around the world as more and more informal public spaces disappear from our real lives. I also suspect that these new media attract colonies of enthusiasts because CMC enables people to do things with each other in new ways, and to do altogether new kinds of things – just as telegraphs, telephones, and televisions did.
>
> (Rheingold, 1995, p.6)

So Rheingold argues forcefully that the Internet reconfigures communication and community and, crucially, in terms of space.

For Rheingold the Internet doesn't just allow connection *across* space, but itself represents a *new* space for association and community. Communities are of interest rather than based on proximate location. Steven Jones refers to Rheingold's vision as

> a kind of ultimate flowering of community, a place ... where individuals shape their own community by choosing which other communities to belong to. ... we will be able to forge our own places from among the many that exist, not by creating new places but by simply choosing from the menu of those available.
>
> (Jones, 1995, p.11)

With the globalization of community, in Rheingold's vision, we shall see the emergence of a shared consciousness, a global civil society.

ACTIVITY 7.2

If you are connected to the Internet, or can get access, perhaps at an Internet café, log on to WELL, the Whole Earth 'Lectronic Link, the Internet community of which Rheingold is a member and about which he writes (http://www.well.com).

How plausible do you find Rheingold's analysis? What do you see as the place in his argument of his values? How does his argument relate to the evidence on Internet usage and interaction?

COMMENT

These are broad questions, but my first response is to want clarification of the term 'community'. Community is a term used with a tremendous diversity of meanings, almost all of them positive, and it has commonly been seen as something which has passed its golden era, as something in decline. However defined, an Internet community seems to me very different from a traditional, face-to-face, geographically based community. The latter, to my mind, involves shared experiences over an extended period of time (in other words, a shared history) by a diversity of people who are characterized by difference as well as similarity, and who interact with each other across a breadth of daily activities. An Internet community, to the contrary, is made up of like-minded individuals who share only a small part of their lives with one another, and who are enjoying a short, transient, association with one another. Signing on to an Internet forum is rather different from the involvement normally undertaken as membership of a local community. Communities of interest, whilst fine if taken as such (for instance, stamp-collecting), are rather different from communities which contribute to social cohesion. These, of course, are issues about Rheingold's explanation, about the relationship of the facts to his theory and, particularly, the coherence of his argument.

Rheingold, however, makes no claims to being a social scientist. His ideas may be stimulating but he has no interest in the relationship of theory to evidence or of fact to argument. He is committed to his subject and a line of argument, but doesn't reflect critically on this commitment and its implications for his analysis. He *does* refer to some of the scholarly literature, for example on community and on the public sphere, but in a rather *ad hoc* and unsustained manner. He makes no pretence of systematic gathering of data, nor that his argument is rooted in data. His ideas and reported experience, however, contextualize the burgeoning literature on Internet communities.

Internet communities, however, are increasingly being researched by social scientists. Elizabeth Reid has researched interaction on multi-user domains (MUDs) – multi-participant systems on the Internet which have a textual interface (Reid, 1995); Shelley Correll provides an ethnographic account of an electronic bar, the lesbian café, created as a computer bulletin board system (BBS) (Correll, 1995); and Ananda Mitra has undertaken research on how the Indian diaspora is connected by the Internet, which we shall examine shortly (Mitra, 1997). In different ways, these and numerous other studies provide evidence of meaningful and somewhat stabilized online communities. Many of these accounts point to the distinctively intimate form of address and communication which takes place in Internet communities. Others, however, argue that such communication is far from community, though is often seen in such terms.

Internet communities (by definition based on interest rather than geographical location) *reduce* the diversity of voices and interests with whom community members interact, and – in that they take us away from local community participation by absorbing our time – they actually lead to a weakening of local community ties or associations. Thus, according to Stephen Doheny-Farina and others, Internet communities, paradoxically, contribute to the *demise* of the public sphere and community (Doheny-Farina, 1996). In short, it is argued that Rheingold's claims are not entirely supported by the evidence, which can be explained in other ways. His argument can be criticized for its limited validity and coherence. Where Rheingold's argument is rooted in his experience and enthusiasm, social scientists look for data on the subject.

3 INTERNET COMMUNITIES CASE STUDY: THE INDIAN USENET

In a less utopian frame than Rheingold, research has documented uses of the Internet to imagine communities and nations. Ananda Mitra, like Rheingold, has an interest in the Internet from his personal use of it. He has undertaken research on an Internet forum on India (Mitra, 1997). *Soc.Culture.Indian* is a **usenet** group to which contributions can be posted by anyone. It also allows cross-postings to other newsgroups, and what is important in this respect with the Indian newsgroup are cross-postings to other countries' newsgroups – especially that for Pakistan. Mitra's research is based on his analysis of the 1,287 postings that were online on the usenet group on a given date in 1995. Most users are situated in the USA, a handful in Western Europe and a few in India.

Usenet
The network of thousands of newsgroups, online CMC communities that are open to anyone with a computer connected to the Internet.

By cross-posting to other usenet groups, the physical boundaries of neighbourhoods or nations can be crossed to areas where contributors simply do not belong. There are no immigration offices or police to prevent such movement. The main participants in the group are bound together by their roots in India, the original home to which they all belonged and the reason for their sense of community. At the same time participants are involved in a new geographical space, the West and particularly the USA, where 'belonging' is more problematic.

Mitra classifies the postings into a number of categories; so his is a form of textual analysis which we discussed in Chapter 5. First, he identifies *general postings*. These are primarily informational, often from someone trying to find someone else. The overlapping interests of users means that they often can and will support one another in this way. 'What these postings indicate is that there is a strong tendency among the subcontinental users to try to find "similar" people who share the histories and practices that produce the communal identity of the users as they exist outside of the network' (Mitra, 1997, p.63). So these postings bring users together.

The second category of postings relate to what Mitra refers to as the *national critical discourse*. These relate to religion and the tensions between various religions that produce contemporary Indian national identity. Discussions are sometimes heated, and topics and positions are many and shifting. For example, one debate concerned the renaming of the commercial centre of Bombay to its pre-British name of Mumbai.

On March 25, 1995 'Krishanan' posted the following:

I realize that the Shiv Sena is changing the name because it the name BOMBAY was christened by foreigners. But the implications are too expensive. All the airlines have to change the name from Bombay to Mumbai ... And all of this for what, it is not going to benefit anybody for changing the name, bcoz the British do not feel slighted by this act, except it might just elicit a few laughs at this jingoistic and brash act.

In response 'Dr Jai Maharaj' wrote:

Send the bill to London. Also, enclose a demand for the return of the Koh-i-noor diamond, all other stolen riches, and just compensation to all victims and their descendants for the British atrocities on the people of Bharat and south Asia.

The piece is signed off with the Hindu greeting 'Om Shanti', which translates to 'Hail Peace'.

(Mitra, 1997, p.65)

Mitra exemplifies his points by citing and discussing such extracts from postings on the newsgroup. In this case he goes on to discuss the diversity of voices which find expression, including those of opinionated bigots.

A third category of postings relates to the role of India and Indians in the culture, society and politics of the West, particularly the USA. For example, there are discussions about the portrayal of an Indian rapist on the television programme *NYPD Blue* and about how Christian television channels talk about the 'pagan' Hindu religion. Interestingly, 'These exchanges work to bring the community together just when discussions about India tend to split the group apart' (Mitra, 1997, pp.66–7).

Mitra provides a plausible analysis and draws some stimulating conclusions. We'll refer to four of these. First, space is critical to the existence of the forum. The loss of geographical proximity is the reason for the use of the Internet space. So this is very different from Rheingold's WELL, which is based in San Francisco's Bay area. In other words, members of the WELL live in geographical proximity to one another in the physical world.

Second is the question of national images. Mitra posits two ways of thinking about these. One is the image produced by organized sources such as the national media, where a monolithic image is constructed for particular political and ideological purposes. The other is the negotiation of their national image by the group most heavily involved with the consequences of this image – immigrants. The Internet provides a forum for developing discourses that allow debate and re-imaging.

Third is the profoundly democratizing nature of the usenet group. The space cannot be co-opted by any one point of view. Compared with other media, power and control is diffused – contrast the usenet with the BBC and public service broadcasting. The cacophony of voices on the Internet makes domination, as traditionally conceived, an impossibility. Notions of gaining consent become irrelevant as traditional centres disappear with the arrival and development of the Internet.

Finally, Mitra raises the dynamic nature of Internet texts and the implications for the researcher. With traditional media, a film for example, there is an 'end' to the text, which in various ways provides a fixed point for analysis.

Contexts of consumption and decoding may vary, but the text remains fixed. With Internet texts, this is simply not the case. All that one can do is to take a snapshot, and acknowledge that the text is ever-metamorphosing and growing. This transient nature of the object of analysis highlights for us the provisional nature of social science understanding.

Let's run our four criteria of evaluation through Mitra's work. The topic of his research, the India usenet forum, is something in which he was involved as a user prior to his research. Such a connection with a research topic is not unusual, and his account shows a transparency about his position and interests. Using textual or discourse analysis, Mitra makes limited claims regarding validity – a notion more applicable to the positivist paradigm. Without a copy of the full transcript of the forum's postings we are not really in a position to comment on the validity of his analysis. Regarding reliability, clearly there is no chance of perfect replication since time (and postings) has moved on, but one might expect a study of a comparable community today to generate similar findings. In the tradition of his chosen method, Mitra makes only limited claims regarding comprehensiveness: he provides an analysis of particular postings to a particular forum at a specific time, making no claims to broader applicability. Coherence in the context of textual analysis relates largely to the *plausibility* of the analysis provided – which depends in part on the professional credibility and integrity of the researcher. Mitra's seems a rigorous study, and he provides an interesting analysis. He employs the qualitative research method of textual analysis. In this context, his analysis and its broader applicability depend very much on his reading and analysis, his professional integrity and the plausibility of his findings.

4   SATELLITE TELEVISION

The other area of research into time–space reconfiguration we'll explore is in media studies, where there is a well-established tradition of audience research exploring how, for example, television is consumed in the home, and how this is shaped by everyday routines and practices. This is highly relevant to some issues we've discussed in this chapter, because broadcasting is one important way in which the *temporal cycle of social life* has been routinized. In the process, broadcasting has became both woven in to, and has constructed, daily life and the annual calendar, *linking the private and the public*. The media theorists Paddy Scannell and David Cardiff describe the significance of this phenomenon:

> A nation, as David Chaney points out, is an abstract collectivity. It is too big to be grasped by individuals. A sense of belonging, the 'we-feeling' of the community, has to be continually engendered by opportunities for identification as the nation is being manufactured. Radio and, later, television were potent means of manufacturing that 'we-feeling'. They made the nation real and tangible through

a whole range of images and symbols, events and ceremonies, relayed to audiences direct and live ...

The cornerstone of the broadcast calendar was the religious year: the weekly observations of the Sabbath through church services and a programme schedule markedly more austere than on other days; the great landmarks of Easter, Pentecost and Christmas; the feast days of the patron saints of England, Scotland and Wales which occasioned special programmes from the appropriate 'region', though what to do with St Patrick's Day was an annually recurring headache for the programme-makers in Belfast. Bank holidays were celebrated in festive mood while the solemn days of national remembrance were marked by religious services and special feature programmes. Sport of course developed its own calendar very quickly. The winter season had its weekly observances of football, rugby, and steeple-chasing, climaxing in the Boat Race, the Grand National and the Cup Final. Summer brought in cricket and flat racing, the test matches, Derby Day, Royal Ascot and Wimbledon.

Threaded through the year was a tapestry of civic, cultural, royal and state occasions: Trooping the Colour, the Ceremony of the Keys, the Lord Mayor's Banquet, the Chairing of the Bard, the Dunmow Flitch, the Shakespeare memorial celebrations at Stratford and much, much more ...

The fireside months were generally better stocked with 'serious' listening matter, but from Whitsun onwards the lighter elements in the programmes were expected to have an increasingly wide appeal. At the same time the broadcasters claimed to have redressed the balance between the seasons of the year, making it possible now to hear good music and plays throughout the summer months when the theatres and concert halls were closed. Thus the programme planners tried to find broadly appropriate material to suit the climate of the year and the mood and leisure activities of the audience. The highpoint of these activities were the annual arrangements for Christmas Day.

(Scannell and Cardiff, 1991, pp.277, 279–80)

Thus, they argue, broadcasting 'unobtrusively stitched together the private and the public spheres' (Scannell and Cardiff, 1991, p.278). Similar processes were underway regarding the rhythm of the day.

Phantasmagoric
Giddens argues that place becomes increasingly 'phantasmagoric' as locales become thoroughly penetrated and shaped by distant social influences – one aspect of the growing separation of place from space.

Today, of course, all this has changed with 24-hour programming, 24-hour news, and a range of niche channels which disrupt this time sequence. Moreover, today it is not just broadcasting but also other ICTs which transform time–space relations, mediating the private world of the home and the public world beyond the doorstep, linking the two spheres and allowing one to communicate with the other. Anthony Giddens has commented on the dramatic increase in the intrusion of distant events into everyday consciousness. As the home becomes increasingly penetrated by distant influences, it becomes what he calls '**phantasmagoric**'. Television brings distant places into our living rooms, and at the same time transports us – in an imaginary rather than physical sense – to faraway places. The growth of processes of **mediation** means that our boundaries of identification and community are extended, and place, where we are, becomes less and less significant for communities (Giddens, 1991).

Shaun Moores is a researcher of media audiences and has undertaken what he refers to as ethnographic research on the consumption of satellite television in South Wales. **Ethnography** is a method with origins in anthropology in the early twentieth century. Malinowski's work on the Trobriand islands and Radcliffe-Brown's on the Andaman islanders are commonly cited as foundational studies (Malinowski, 1922; Radcliffe-Brown, 1948). Ethnography is based on the *in situ* observation of a group over an extended period of time; a year or more of fieldwork is not uncommon. The ethnographer spends their time observing and participating in the everyday activities of the group, recording fieldnotes in writing and using audio- and video-tape recorders. In addition, loose, unstructured or semi-structured interviews are undertaken with informants. The intention is to make sense of social interaction in participants' terms, in other words, to understand a culture as its members do or, as Malinowski (1922, ch.1) put it, to understand 'the native's point of view'. Of course, it is naïve to think it possible to have some complete knowledge of such an 'other': ethnographic discourses are always and necessarily partial truths, and what is being described is at least in part a product of the researcher's imagination and language. This has led to a strand of ethnography which emphasizes these subjective aspects of the research process, and focuses on reflexivity, which for some researchers has become almost the main focus of their writing. Despite such a position, ethnography as description of something 'out there' has become increasingly popular as a research method, commonly deployed today in the developed world.

In fact, and as he acknowledges, Moores' work is rather different from ethnography as commonly understood and practised (Moores, 1996). It shares the theoretical concerns of classical ethnography but practices these by means of interviews in respondents' homes, albeit interviews which are semi-structured and follow the tenets and format of **ethnographic interviews**. Moores is concerned with situated, everyday practices, but immersed himself for only a couple of hours, albeit 2 hours in which he is sympathetic to respondents' understandings and categories. On occasions Moores refers to his cases as '**ethnographic portraits**'.

In the early 1990s Moores visited 18 households which displayed satellite dishes – then a new phenomenon. At the outset he had a specific set of concerns: to explore the diversity of ways in which satellite television was being appropriated and interpreted in different settings; and how it was used to articulate particular social relations or divisions of class, race, generation and ethnicity. In other words, he had a set of theoretical or conceptual concerns which he wanted to explore, and he chose to do this qualitatively and in relation to what was then an exciting new media technology, satellite television. He selected three contrasting neighbourhoods, and each of the

Mediation
Our understanding of the world is increasingly mediated as symbolic forms replace personal experience (and that of others handed down through face-to-face interaction).

Ethnography
Ethnography is a qualitative, reflexive, approach to social research, developed by anthropologists, that uses a range of data sources but has at its heart participation by the researcher in everyday life for an extended period of time.

Ethnographic interviews
Ethnographic interviews explore issues in which the ethnographer is interested, but do not involve predetermined questions. Questions are often open-ended or non-directive, but might be directive or specific, for example when testing an emerging hypothesis.

Ethnographic portraits
Media researchers' ethnographic portraits are qualitative accounts of households and their media, drawing mainly on interviews. They may draw also on some observation and time-use diaries, but are not based on extensive participant observation or ethnography.

18 interviews lasted up to 2 hours. In the tradition of ethnographic interviewing, interviews were semi-structured, and respondents were encouraged to speak from their experience. Questions were open-ended, but he kept a mental checklist of topics to be covered. He does not tell us how he recorded or analysed the interviews, though the data he cites suggest that his interviews were recorded and transcribed in some way. He refers to making notes afterwards about domestic layout and household dynamics.

Normally, social scientists provide more detail about their research methods to allow some possibility for other researchers to evaluate their claims, to see the extent to which their work meets the canons of social science research regarding validity, reliability, comprehensiveness and coherence. First, let's explore the nature of such **semi-structured interviews**. The normal format is for the researcher to begin with a checklist of questions, topics, or areas that they are interested in exploring with interviewees. These are likely to be derived from issues raised by the literature and a theoretical position. Moores, for example, as a researcher of media audiences, takes up well-rehearsed debates about time–space relations and domestic power and politics, and applies these to what was then a new topic, satellite television. A semi-structured interview is non-directive and allows the interviewee to speak for themselves, to enable the researcher to understand the categories and meanings of the actor rather than (as in a questionnaire, for example) to impose those of the researcher. During the interview, the interviewer will allow the interview to take as 'natural' a course as possible, occasionally directing the conversation to topics or questions on the checklist, but as unobtrusively as possible. At the end of the interview, everything on the checklist has to be covered, but not in any particular order, or in an identical format or form of questioning as for other interviewees. Commonly, interviews are tape-recorded; in other settings, notes are made, usually at the time or, in more sensitive contexts, immediately after the interview. The idea is that written notes should be as verbatim as possible, and that they should use the language and expressions of respondents, not some reported or translated version of this. This allows the voice of the interviewee to be reported.

The other aspect of Moores' work is his observation of households. This is a tradition of research rooted in the **participant observation** of the Chicago School of sociology in the 1930s. At the time a radical departure, their concern was with understanding the life of the underclass. To investigate this members of the Chicago School sought to develop an understanding of how drug addicts, prostitutes, jazz musicians, hoboes and others made sense of the world, and got by in their everyday lives. Rather than moralistic or judgemental, their concern was to identify the perceptions and understandings of those they were studying. Participant observation is commonly understood as taking place somewhere on a spectrum from 'full participation', when the researcher behaves as, to all intents and purposes, a member of, for example, the religious sect they are researching, to more detached observation. Moores' observation seems nearer the latter: his

Semi-structured interviews

A semi-structured interview usually explores topics rather than involving standardized questions. It is reflexive, and questions are non-directive and open-ended.

Participant observation

Participant observation is a research method involving fieldwork. It ranges between full participation in the research setting and more detached observation.

account of his methods gives no indication that he observed family television viewing, or that he participated in their leisure activities.

Other audience researchers have done so, notably Marie Gillespie, who studied young Punjabis' uses of video in Southall in the 1980s (Gillespie, 1995). Gillespie's work is ethnographic in the anthropological tradition. She immersed herself in the field for a period of several years, she learnt Punjabi, and her account is rooted in the 'thick description' which characterizes ethnographic research. Ethnography is an approach to research which is concerned with the perspectives and understandings of those researched. It draws on data from various sources (including documents and perhaps even questionnaires) but with in-depth, sustained fieldwork at its core; and it involves a particular form of writing, with writing-up beginning as the data are being gathered, as ideas are emerging, and in a way which gives a voice to those who are being researched. Commonly, preliminary findings are subject to '**respondent validation**' by being taken to respondents for their comment on whether it seems to be 'telling the story as it is'.

Whether participation, observation, or ethnography, fieldwork involves the negotiation of access. Moores describes how he identified houses with satellite dishes and wrote to their occupants on an official letterhead, asking if he could interview them for his research. He then visited them for an evening. In other contexts, negotiation of access is not something undertaken at the outset and then completed, but is more of an on-going matter. For example, researching in a pub might involve gaining the approval of the landlord in the first instance, but would fairly soon involve negotiation with 'regulars', and even then, on an on-going basis, would involve explaining one's interests and concerns to newcomers.

Respondent validation
Respondent validation is a way of testing the researcher's analysis, to see whether those purportedly described recognize the validity of the account. It can be treated as an additional source of data.

This raises an important ethical issue of what constitutes a sufficient explanation of one's research interest. On the one hand, few in a pub will want to know the hypothesis on time–space reconfiguration which you are interested in exploring. On the other hand, to undertake covert research, where those being researched are unaware that this is the case, is justifiable in only the most extreme circumstances; for example, an obscure or extreme religious sect which would not otherwise allow access. Such instances are few, and covert research is a serious ethical issue among social scientists.

Linked to the negotiation of access is the question of conduct in the field. Broadly speaking, in undertaking qualitative fieldwork, the researcher should remain as unobtrusive as possible, to restrict as fully as possible the impact of the observer on the setting. So dress and behaviour should conform as closely as possible to the norm of the setting.

Having addressed the nature and some issues about research methods, we'll return to Moores' work on satellite television. We'll confine our attention to two of the interviews which Moores reports. First is the Gibson family, living in an Edwardian bay-fronted neighbourhood 5 km from the city centre. Moores describes the taste of Mr Gibson, who appreciates the 'character' and heritage value of his property. Whilst Mr Gibson indulges in his antique restoration, his son – at whose request the satellite dish was acquired – is ensconced in the attic. The third member of the household, Mrs Gibson, hardly appears in the account, though we're told that Tony, the son, inherited from her his taste for 1960s music.

ACTIVITY 7.3

Read the following extract from Moores' work on the Gibson family. As you do so, note what it indicates about space and place. How does satellite television, in mediating between the household and the outside world, reinforce or transform notions of space and time?

> At the top of the house, separated from the main living area by a narrow staircase and landing, is Tony's room. He is intensely proud of this space and the objects arranged in it – regarding the attic as a place into which he can retreat, and as a symbol of independence from the rest of the family. Showing me around the room, Tony explains:
>
>> I'm the only one who knows how to use any of my electrical equipment. Nobody else comes in my room – I think of it as my space ... Up here, I can watch anything I want, read, sleep, think about life, listen to music ... As soon as I go into my room, it's like I'm on another planet.
>
> Gathered around his television set, there is a remarkable entourage of technical hardware and software – as well as an array of decorative images and artefacts. Two video recorders, a hi-fi system and the satellite receiver are all stacked on shelves underneath the TV. They have been wired together, too, so that the sound comes out of four Dolby surround speakers mounted on brackets in each corner of the room ...
>
> Tony's positive feelings about the Astra broadcasts – he tunes in to continental stations like RTL Plus or Pro 7, as well as the Sky channels and MTV Europe – are intimately related to his dismissal of established terrestrial programming as traditional, boring and old fashioned. In fact, it is interesting that he labels this negatively as 'British television'. Mr and Mrs Gibson use precisely the same label themselves, but here its value is completely reversed. They prefer to watch BBC or ITV in the living room downstairs.
>
> (Moores, 1996, pp.37–8, 40)

C O M M E N T

This extract from Moores' account of the Gibson household tells us about domestic space – how new media technologies are central to defining the son's space, activity and identity. It also demonstrates how satellite television (or Astra broadcasting, to be precise) allows Tony to enjoy non-British television, to take him beyond the confines of British broadcasting.

The Harveys live nearby. They are in their twenties and have three young children. Dave Harvey works for his own business and is an electronics graduate. Again, Moores reports his interview with the male adult of the household, who suggests that satellite television enables him to travel to new places and to re-imagine the boundaries of community.

ACTIVITY 7.4

As you read the following extract from Moores' account of the Harvey household, consider whether the evidence he cites is sufficient for his argument that this is a re-imagined community. Might the data generate alternative explanations?

> Mr Harvey, who manufactures hi-tech goods for the export market, already identifies strongly with a transnational business community. The fact that his parents have bought a retirement home in Spain contributes to Dave's recognition of himself as 'a European'. Their villa is now a regular destination for family holidays abroad. Mrs Harvey, too, finds the idea of Europe has a certain limited salience. When her younger sister – a university arts student – came to visit with a boyfriend from France, they were able to show them a few French language programmes on satellite television ...

> Mr Harvey explains that:

>> When I'm watching Sky – because it's from a European satellite – and when I'm looking at some of the other continental stations that are available, I very much get the sense of being a European. A lot of the channels are an hour ahead, they're on European time. If you're just channel-hopping, which is a bit of a sport for me – buzzing round eight or nine stations to see what's going on – you do get the feeling of not being restricted in the good old British way. It's quite something when you can sit down in your own front room and watch what's on in another country.

> (Moores, 1996, p.41)

C O M M E N T

Again, Moores points to how satellite television is implicated in processes of identification. In mediating the boundary between private lives and public culture, the technology has implications for identities.

However, it's quite unusual in the UK to find people who identify themselves as 'European', even if they are sympathetic to the EU and the 'project' of Europe. It's also unusual for someone to choose to view national television produced in another country; most of the television programming which crosses national borders successfully is from the USA. One reason for this is that, particularly in Europe, different languages are spoken in different countries. Does Mr Harvey *speak* foreign languages? If so, how much is the television the cause as opposed to manifestation of his Europeanness? Given these issues, I was left doubting the validity or depth of Mr Harvey's account of his rationale for his television viewing preferences.

Like Mitra, Moores provides a qualitative account of an ICT and its role in mediation and community. His research method is a qualitative one, the semi-structured interview, a technique which ethnographers deploy. Unlike an ethnographer, however, Moores did not undertake extended fieldwork. So his data (and hence analysis) remain very much rooted in respondents' *accounts* of their actions and motivations – on what they *say* they do. That his data are reported can be seen as limiting their validity. Qualitative interviews are a much quicker research method, and hence allow a greater breadth of cases to be examined. Moores' work provides some qualitative richness and depth, but less than would be provided by the in-depth, sustained, fieldwork of the ethnographer.

5   CONCLUSION

In this chapter we have discussed aspects of time–space reconfiguration which are important for understanding contemporary social transformations. Such debates can be taken back to the onset of industrialization (or earlier) and to the development of a succession of technologies (for example, the telegraph in the nineteenth century). They have acquired a much-heightened significance with the onset of digital communications and, in particular, the Internet. It would be hard to deny some dramatic reconfiguration of time and space in recent years. The significance of these processes, however, is more debatable.

As we saw in Chapter 2, Castells' account of the network society is a macro analysis, albeit one which links issues of economic restructuring and new communication technologies with questions of identity. We discussed problems regarding the relationship between theory and evidence in Castells' work, and suggested that a major strength is the comprehensiveness of his argument. His phenomenal reputation worldwide may testify to this, to the applicability and relevance of his argument to all sectors and societies.

In contrast with Castells' macro view, in this chapter we have explored more micro research studies that provide data and analysis relating to processes of time–space reconfiguration. These complement Castells' work, which is rooted in quantitative data and official statistics. They are qualitative studies and provide a richness and depth of data regarding more specific phenomena or settings.

Although Mitra and Moores are interested in broader issues – including diaspora identities and mediated modernity – their claims and arguments rest on their specific case studies or 'ethnographic portraits'. As with all research, this raises questions about the relationship of theory to data. Each of them focuses very much on the specific research setting, describing it in qualitative terms, quoting verbatim, and letting the subjects of their research 'speak for themselves'. In this, of course, there is a difference between Mitra's discourse analysis and Moores' semi-structured interviews.

Moores seems to start with theoretical interests, but his data do not lead him to modify any arguments about mediation or time–space. Rather, they illustrate the analysis he provided at the outset – bringing this to life, and applying it to a new technology, satellite television.

Mitra's textual analysis seems more exploratory and, in a sense, more open. But it is rooted in his assumptions about meanings and readings. His analysis seems more driven by data than is Moores' – his classification and discussion of postings emerged from his data. Yet, like Moores, Mitra links the data with broader conceptual or theoretical concerns, notably national identity.

Both, however, are valuable as qualitative explorations of specific settings in which we can explore time–space reconfiguration, and as examples of how social scientists undertake research on the information society.

Conclusion

Hugh Mackay

1   SOCIAL SCIENCE RESEARCH

In this book we have explored aspects of the information society to introduce and explain the nature of social science research. We have discussed some important social transformations that are underway, and have introduced some core issues, principles and practices of social research. The social changes we have discussed are commonly explained by all manner of politicians, policy makers, journalists and other commentators. We have argued that social science is distinguished from other arguments and explanations in that it is rooted in a set of principles and practices.

Social science argument and explanation derive from the researcher (their identity, predispositions and preferences), the theories in which they are interested (and which they apply and develop) and the data (that they gather or use). Social scientists evaluate their own and one another's work in terms of its validity, reliability, comprehensiveness and coherence – criteria that apply to both data and argument.

Within the social sciences there are numerous perspectives and methodologies. We have outlined, in Chapter 4, something of a historical trajectory of methodology. We introduced positivism, and its emergence in the nineteenth century as an attempt to construct a science of society analogous to the natural sciences. Many of the early sociologists – Auguste Comte, Emile Durkheim and Herbert Spencer – had backgrounds in the natural sciences or mathematics and sought to develop a science of society which had the rigour of natural science, seeing social science as concerned with establishing the natural laws of society.

Interpretivism developed as social science faculties became established in universities, and a professional cadre of social scientists began to explore the differences between societies and between people. It came from a growing awareness that the social facts of positivism could not explain adequately the diversity of ways in which societies worked. Interpretivists developed methods to gather data from people – the rich diversity of people who lie behind official statistics. They developed frameworks to order these data and to portray their meanings. These frameworks drew more from philosophy and the humanities than the scientific model of positivism.

Critical methodologies are rooted in acknowledgement of some underlying, structured, patterning of society. Critical theorists have been concerned to address structured inequalities, to explore in diverse ways how these are sustained and transformed, and how they constrain individuals and provide a framework for their daily lives.

Most recently we have seen the development of cultural approaches which can be seen as an attempt to explain the emerging information society. Cultural approaches raise two main issues that seem helpful. First is that growing cultural diversity and globalization means the end of any meta narrative, of the possibility of any one overarching theory explaining everything. Social science, it is argued, can provide only a modest contribution to understanding, given the limits of the grand theories of (say) class and gender. The annihilation of time and space means a world of endless change and complexity. Second is the focus on representation and identity: with the massive growth of the media and of representational practices we can see how meanings – and reality – are constructed and contested. This leads to a shift of focus from structures and institutions to discourses and identities.

Thus positivist, interpretive, critical and cultural methodologies have each challenged and extended social science thinking and method. A major impetus to this development of social theory has been debates about methodology and what constitutes evidence and argument in the social sciences – from the positivist social fact to the cultural discourse.

We have seen how methodologies are associated with particular methods, or techniques, of social research. In the last three chapters we have introduced a number of important qualitative and quantitative research methods, including textual and discourse analysis (Chapter 5), statistical tests (Chapter 6) and observation and semi-structured interviews (Chapter 7). Such methods are selected on the basis of the researcher's methodology, the nature of the subject of their research, and the data that are available or might be collected. Each is selected on the basis of an understanding of its strengths and limits. Social research, however, is a much more complex process than following a cook book, commonly involving negotiation, judgement and compromise in the collection and analysis of data and the development of argument.

Social scientists' research is evaluated in terms of the four criteria we have identified – validity, reliability, comprehensiveness and coherence. The meaning and significance of each of these varies according to the methodology. Despite this variety, they remain the criteria whereby claims to truth and utility are established in the social sciences.

One important change with social research in the information society is that, with new ICTs, the amount of information available and the technical possibilities for gathering and processing this have increased dramatically. An e-mail questionnaire can reach a large population at little cost. It is possible to interview people around the world, and even to see them as well, through video-conferencing technology. An ever-increasing array of data archives, library materials and other information sources can be accessed electronically and remotely.

At the same time, social research becomes more complex. Greater volumes of data are available, but often with less sense of how to evaluate their reliability or validity. The virtuality of intervention requires new ways of understanding, as well as making more complex the tasks of describing and evaluating.

Whilst research subjects have changed, and research methods change or are used differently, the central issues of social science research and argument endure. The information society will not bring a more certain truth about human behaviour and societies – indeed, it appears to be the catalyst for the use of a greater diversity of methods to understand more complex and faster changing social issues.

2   UNDERSTANDING TECHNOLOGICAL CHANGE

If there is one core issue in our discussion of information society debates it is the limits of the technological determinism that characterizes so much of the debates. Social science is concerned with exploring the complexity of social processes, which tends to contrast with other commentaries. In essence, the argument of social scientists is that technologies are shaped by the social. By focusing on the myriad of ways in which technology is shaped by society, social science positions us in a less passive role vis-à-vis technology: it is people and societies that make choices about the development and uses of technologies.

We have identified three core themes in information society debates: culture, representation and identities; changing patterns of work and inequality; and time–space reconfiguration. Each could be explored using any research method, and a vast amount of research is undertaken on each. We selected studies that would allow us to introduce a range of methods and, at the same time, were studies of subjects that allowed us to develop substantively each of these three themes of information society debates. Whereas Bell and Castells provide us with very broad accounts of social transformation, most of the studies we have explored are more modest in their scope and claims. Nonetheless, they capture some aspect of the theme in question, and make an important contribution to debates and understanding. By exploring substantive arguments at the same time as their particular research methods, we have identified some of the issues and limits of both research methods and social science argument.

From the breadth of studies we have introduced we can identify three themes. First is the tension between theory and data. In relation to most theory we can identify data that are supportive, but also data that counter the theory. Some research does little more than illustrate a theory or concept. Other research is characterized by more iteration between the two – perhaps involving some refinement of the theory in the light of the empirical findings.

Many explanations of the information society are broad in scope – so need more data to be sustained. More restricted themes might be more easily explored empirically, and might allow more interplay between data and argument.

Second is the subjective nature of social research. In the research we have explored we have seen how the methods used and arguments developed have been shaped, in part, by the values, theoretical position and experience of the researcher. Today few claim value-freedom, while considerable attention is given to subjectivity and reflexivity in research. This does not negate, but makes more complex, the criteria whereby we can evaluate research.

Finally, our discussion of this research suggests that social science does not provide any clear, unequivocal or uncontested account of social change. In an ever more complex and fast-changing world, social science explanation and understanding is always incomplete.

The reason we do social science, notwithstanding these problems, is that social science gives us insight into social processes, structures and agency. It provides us with the theory and methods for understanding the information society.

References

Adbusters, at www.adbusters.org (accessed 6 November 2000).

Atkinson, M. (2000) 'Poor need penicillin before Pentiums', *The Guardian*, 28 August.

Bangemann, M. (1994) *Europe and the Global Information Society*, recommendations to the European Council, Brussels, EC.

Barnes, B. and Edge, D. (eds) (1982) *Science in Context*, Milton Keynes, Open University Press.

Barthes, R. (1972) *Mythologies*, Paris, Seuil.

Bauman, Z. (1990) *Thinking Sociologically*, Oxford, Blackwell.

Bell, D. (1974) *The Coming of Post-Industrial Society: A Venture in Social Forecasting*, London, Heinemann (first published New York, Basic Books, 1973).

Bell, D. (1980) 'The social framework of the information society' in Forester, T. (ed.) *The Microelectronics Revolution*, Oxford, Blackwell.

Bolter, J.D. (1986) *Turing's Man*, Harmondsworth, Penguin (first published North Carolina University Press, 1984).

Bowers, N. and Martin, J.P. (2000) 'Going mobile? Jobs in the new economy', OECD, at www.oecdobserver.org/news/fullstory.php/aid/319 (accessed 21 November 2000).

Braverman, H. (1974) *Labor and Monopoly Capital: The Degradation of Work in the Twentieth Century*, New York, Monthly Review Press.

Bulmer, M. (1984) 'Introduction – problems, theories and methods in sociology – (how) do they interrelate?' in Bulmer, M. (ed.) *Sociological Research Methods: An Introduction*, London, Macmillan.

Castells, M. (1996) *The Rise of the Network Society. The Information Age: Economy, Society and Culture*, Vol.1, Oxford, Blackwell.

Castells, M. (1997) *The Power of Identity. The Information Age: Economy, Society and Culture*, Vol.2, Oxford, Blackwell.

Castells, M. (1998) *End of Millennium. The Information Age: Economy, Society and Culture*, Vol.3, Oxford, Blackwell.

Castells, M. (1999) 'An introduction to the information age' in Mackay, H. and O'Sullivan, T. (eds) *The Media Reader: Continuity and Transformation*, London, Sage.

Chandler, D. and Roberts-Young, D. (1998) 'The construction of identity in the personal homepages of adolescents', at http://www.aber.ac.uk/media/Documents/short/strasbourg.html (accessed 22 October 2000).

Cheung, C. (2000) 'A home on the web: presentation of self on personal homepages' in Gauntlett, D. (ed.) (2000) *Web.Studies: Rewiring Media Studies for the Digital Age*, London, Arnold.

Collinson, P. (2000) 'Are you billed as a villain in the X-files?', *The Guardian*, Jobs and Money section, 16 September, pp.2–3.

Correll, S. (1995) 'The ethnography of an electronic bar, The Lesbian Café', *Journal of Contemporary Ethnography*, vol.24, no.3, pp.270–98.

Cowan, R.S. (1995) 'How the refrigerator got its hum' in MacKenzie, D. and Wajcman, J. (eds).

Department of Trade and Industry (2000) *Closing the Digital Divide: Information and Communication Technologies in Deprived Areas*, a report by Policy Action Team 15, DTI.

Doheny-Farina, S. (1996) *The Wired Neighbourhood*, New Haven, Yale University Press.

Duff, A. (1998) 'Daniel Bell's theory of the information society', *Journal of Information Science*, vol.2, no.6, pp.373–93.

Duff, A. and McCleery, A. (1996) 'The evolving European information society', *Scottish Communication Association Journal*, vol.2, pp.157–75.

Durkheim, E. (1895/1966) *The Rules of Sociological Method*, London, Free Press.

Foucault, M. (1977) *Discipline and Punish: The Birth of the Prison*, London, Penguin.

Gershuny, J. and Miles, I. (1983) *The New Service Economy: The Transformation of Employment in Industrial Societies*, London, Pinter.

Giddens, A. (1984) *The Constitution of Society*, Cambridge, Polity.

Giddens, A. (1990) *The Consequences of Modernity*, Cambridge, Polity.

Giddens, A. (1991) *Modernity and Self Identity: Self and Society in the Late Modern Age*, Cambridge, Polity.

Gillespie, M. (1995) *Television, Ethnicity and Cultural Change*, London, Routledge.

Goldblatt, D. (ed.) (2000) *Knowledge and the Social Sciences: Theory, Method, Practice*, London, Routledge/The Open University.

Gouldner, A. (1971) *The Coming Crisis in Western Sociology*, London, Heinemann.

Hakken, D. (1999) *Cyborgs @ Cyberspace, An Ethnographer Looks to the Future*, New York, Routledge.

Hall, S. (1992) 'The West and the rest' in Hall, S. and Gieben, B. (eds) *Formations of Modernity*, Cambridge, Polity/The Open University.

Hall, S. (1997a) 'The work of representation' in Hall, S. (ed.).

Hall, S. (1997b) 'The spectacle of the "other"' in Hall, S. (ed.).

Hall, S. (ed.) (1997) *Representation: Cultural Representations and Signifying Practices*, London, Sage/The Open University.

Harvey, D. (1990) *The Condition of Postmodernity*, Oxford, Blackwell.

Hayward, T. (2000) 'The question is, what's in it for me?', *The Guardian*, 30 October, Media section, p.54.

Hobsbawn, E. (1995) *The Age of Extremes, A History of the World, 1914–91*, New York, Vintage.

Independent Television Commission (1999) *Television: The Public's View 1998*, London, ITC.

International Labour Office (1999) *Yearbook of Labour Statistics*, Geneva, ILO.

Jameson, F. (1984) 'Postmodernism, or the cultural logic of late capitalism', *New Left Review*, vol.146, pp.53–92.

Jameson, F. (1991) *Postmodernism or the Cultural Logic of Late Capitalism*, London, Verso.

Jones, S.G. (1995) 'Understanding community in the information age' in Jones, S.G. (ed.).

Jones, S.G. (ed.) (1995) *Cybersociety. Computer-mediated Communication and Community*, London, Sage.

Kelso, P. and Adams, G. (2000) 'As one in four homes go online, the country's digital divide widens', *The Guardian*, 11 July, p.3.

Lerner, D. (2000) 'Divide or deluge? Digital revolution splits analysts', *Financial Times*, 27 April.

MacKenzie, D. and Wajcman, J. (1995) 'Introductory essay' in MacKenzie, D. and Wajcman, J. (eds).

MacKenzie, D. and Wajcman, J. (eds) (1995) *The Social Shaping of Technology*, Milton Keynes, Open University Press.

McLuhan, M. (1964) *Understanding Media*, London, Routledge and Kegan Paul.

Malinowski, B. (1922) *Argonauts of the Western Pacific*, London, Routledge and Kegan Paul.

Marx, K. and Engels, F. (1932/1998) *The German Ideology*, London, Elecbook.

May, T. and Williams, M. (1998) *Knowing the Social World*, Buckingham, Open University Press.

Mitra, A. (1997) 'Virtual commonality: looking for India on the Internet' in Jones, S.G. (ed.) *Virtual Culture. Identity and Communication in Cybersociety*, London, Sage.

Moores, S. (1996) *Satellite Television and Everyday Life, Articulating Technology*, Acamedia Research Monograph 18, Luton, John Libbey Media.

Murdock, G. and Golding, P. (1989) 'Information poverty and political inequality: citizenship in the age of privatized communications', *Journal of Communication*, vol.39, no.3, pp.180–95.

Naisbett, J. (1982) *Megatrends: Ten New Directions Transforming Our Lives*, New York, Warner Communications.

Negroponte, N. (1995) *Being Digital*, London, Hodder & Stoughton.

Panos Communications and Social Change Programme (1998) *The Internet and Poverty*, Briefing Paper no.28, London, Panos.

Polsky, N. (1971) *Hustlers, Beats and Others*, Harmondsworth, Penguin.

Poster, M. (1984) *Foucault, Marxism and History*, Cambridge, Polity.

Poster, M. (1990) *The Mode of Information*, Cambridge, Polity.

Radcliffe-Brown, A.R. (1948) *The Andaman Islanders*, Glencoe, Illinois, Free Press.

Reid, E. (1995) 'Virtual worlds: culture and imagination' in Jones, S.G. (ed.).

Rheingold, H. (1995) *The Virtual Community*, London, Minerva (first published in the UK by Secker and Warburg, 1994).

Robins, K. (1995) 'Cyberspace and the world we live in' in Featherstone, M. and Burrows, R. (eds) (1995) *Cyberspace, Cyberbodies, Cyberpunk: Cultures of Technological Embodiment*, London, Sage.

Robins, K. and Webster, F. (1999) *Times of the Technoculture. From the Information Society to the Virtual Life*, London, Routledge.

Scannell, P. and Cardiff, D. (1991) *A Social History of British Broadcasting, Vol.1, 1922–1939*, Oxford, Blackwell.

Sennett, R. (1998) *Corrosion of Character: The Personal Consequences of Work in the New Capitalism*, New York, Norton.

Shapin, S. (1982) 'History of science and its sociological reconstructions', *History of Science*, vol.20, pp.157–211.

Social Trends, London, HMSO (annual).

Soja, E. (1989) *Post-modern Geographics: The Reassertion of Space in Critical Social Theory*, London, Verso.

Stanley, L. and Wise, S. (1993) *Breaking Out Again: Feminist Ontology and Epistemology*, London, Routledge.

Stonier, T. (1983) 'The impact of microprocessors on employment' in Forester, T. (ed.) *The Microelectronics Revolution*, Oxford, Blackwell.

Thompson, E.P. (1967) 'Time, work-discipline and industrial capitalism', *Past and Present*, vol.38, pp.56–97.

Tobin, A. (2000) 'When novelty doesn't work', *The Guardian*, 30 October, Media section.

Toffler, A. (1980) *The Third Wave*, London, Pan.

Turkle, S. (1996a) 'Virtuality and its discontents: searching for community in cyberspace', *The American Prospect*, no.24, winter, at http://www.prospect.org/archives/24/24turk.html (accessed 20 October 2000).

Turkle, S. (1996b) *Life on the Screen: Identity in the Age of the Internet*, London, Weidenfeld & Nicolson.

United Nations Development Programme (1999) *Human Development Report*, Oxford University Press, at http://www.undp.org/hdro/ (accessed January 2001).

Ward, L. (2000) 'Blair says Internet must not remain preserve of elite', *The Guardian*, 6 March.

Webster, F. (1995) *Theories of the Information Society*, London, Routledge.

White, L. (1978) *Medieval Technology and Social Change*, New York, Oxford University Press (first published 1962).

Acknowledgements

Grateful acknowledgement is made to the following sources for permission to reproduce material in this book.

Tables

Table 1.1: *Television: The Public's View 1999*, pp.6–7, © Independent Television Commission; Table 2.1: Bell, D. (1980) 'The social framework of the information society' in Forester, T. (ed.) *The Microelectronics Revolution*, Blackwell Publishers Ltd./by permission of MIT Press; Tables 6.1 and 6.2: Department of Trade and Industry, 2000; Table 6.6: British Social Attitudes (1996) National Centre for Social Research; Table 6.7: *Social Trends* 30, National Statistics © Crown Copyright 2001.

Figures

Figure 2.1: Bell, D. (1980) 'The social framework of the information society' in Forester, T. (ed.) *The Microelectronics Revolution*, Blackwell Publishers Ltd./by permission of MIT Press; Figure 5.1: Courtesy of Hewlett Packard; Figure 6.1: *Social Trends* 30, National Statistics © Crown Copyright 2001; Figure 7.1: Courtesy of Stephen G. Eick, Naperville, IL, USA.

Every effort has been made to trace all the copyright owners, but if any has been inadvertently overlooked, the publishers will be pleased to make the necessary arrangements at the first opportunity.

Index